MW01200543

APOSTOLIC GUIDELINES TO RELEASE THE PROPHETIC

Apostolic Guidelines to Release the Prophetic

Back when I was still a rather novice Pastor in Guam, a well-known minister called me on the phone and invited me to come preach at a Pastor's Conference he was having in the States. His voice was loud and direct and I was very intimidated by this opportunity – having never spoken in a Church in the Continental US before – let alone to a large group of Pastors!

Feeling overwhelmed and amazed by the opportunity, I hung up the phone and put my head down on my desk to ponder the moment. In a flash, I saw a picture of disruption that was happening at his church and neon lights above it with an unknown name – that I wrote down. At that point, this was an unusual experience for me.

The time came for the Conference and after the arduous 21 hour flight, this Minister picked me up at the airport and drove me to the hotel. After sitting in the car and visiting for quite a long time, I finally worked up the nerve to very hesitantly tell him what I had seen – and about the neon light with a lady's name who was causing him turmoil in his church.

Well, this minister seemed *very* upset with me telling him that. He stomped around to my door and put my luggage on the curbside. Leaving me shaking, embarrassed, and all alone – he sped away without a word. His tires were smoldering as his car squealed out of the driveway.

All afternoon, I was totally devastated. Why did I make a fool out of myself? Why would I presume to tell him something so improbable? I was mortified to have dared to speak to him about his Church and people that I didn't know him. I could barely breathe...

Someone else drove me to the service that night, and he didn't look at me or speak to me. And all these strange ministers were there – who I didn't know. I'd been learning to pastor in isolation on an island far from any mentoring and training. Had joined this group to have some relationship with other pastors.

After the song service, this minister he gets up and his voice rumbles the floor with depth and authority, "You guys all go around thinking you hear from God – and I'm here to say that often you don't."

Well... my heart sank. It felt like he was going to rebuke me in public – right then. My heart raced and I wanted to just pass out and then be carried away!

He went on about false prophecy and the misuse of Gifts. "Oh My God..." I thought, "It's really all over for me."

Then he said, "This morning, this woman (pointing to me, gulp) – she told me something that I knew wasn't true. I've been furious all day. Yes, she named the person whom she never met, and I knew *that* wasn't right."

"And then, I went to our church and discussed it with my elders. We found out what she said was true... Now, this trouble maker has been released from our ministry. So now, here is the spokesman with the sure Word of God, all the way from Guam! I'm telling you, you can rely on what she says. Let's welcome her tonight...."

Obviously by now, I could hardly stand – I was in another realm!

* * *

As a result of "learning the hard way" in the prophetic, writing this book became necessary to me. Hopefully, you won't have to learn the hard way!

It is important to understand the various ways that God leads. You need to know that you can communicate this leading in various ways, and you need to find the best way to interpret and deliver what the Lord shows you.

Because each of you is uniquely different, it's useless to try and spiritually connect to God or express what He says in the same manner as someone else. You and I are different because of Divine purpose! God uses your distinctiveness and how you convey your impressions in order to express Himself more fully.

It's sad that many organizations don't encourage believers to try and release what The Lord is saying to them. In reading all these guidelines, please know that the intention is to encourage and train others to bring forth their Gifts in the most accurate way and to bless the Body of Christ. While religion would hamper and separate, Grace and love encourage and protect.

You and I can learn from each other. The way each of us interpret the supernatural signals is unique and NOT standard. This book on protocol is written to find the standards that we can share. Remembering that Divine methods of communication can be as infinite as the Creator desires.

Dr. Kluane

A STATEMENT OF POLICY & PROTOCOL

Enhancing your Prophetic Gift

By Dr. Kluane Spake

The WIND blows where it wishes, and you hear the sound of it, but cannot tell where it comes from and where it goes... So is everyone who is born of the Spirit (Jn. 3:8).

Prophecy is as old as the Bible. Yet many don't understand–or even recognize–when and how it happens today. Taking an apostolic look at the prophetic gives a slightly different view than normally heard.

As you go through this book you will discover that God is speaking to you in the NOW, the Present and wanting you to put words and action to your faith.

Today, the Church is positioned on the periphery of what will go down in church history as a most powerful move of God. It is all about the apostolic government of the Church arising and taking it's place.

This book is about obtaining a greater force of RESULTS from the prophetic. The prophetic gift should be cherished, encouraged, and enhanced. All who are filled with the Spirit can and should participate in the *"spirit of prophecy."*

Now when we talk about prophesying here, it's not about you going up to some stranger and shouting that in 5 minutes their house will catch on fire! (This is not as ridiculous at it may sound – I know someone who did that!)

Nor are we concerned with endless end time events, or "rapture" dates, or disasters, or who the antichrist may be today. What we want to learn is how to 'de-mystify' prophesying and know how to use it effectively.

AN APOSTOLIC KINGDOM VIEW OF THE PROPHETIC

The Church is built on the foundation of apostles and prophets! (Eph. 2:20, Gal. 2:20). God GAVE (and keeps on giving) some (not all) apostles and some (not all) prophets.

1 Corinthians 12:28 explains, "And God has set *some* in the church FIRST (first sent, first one in, first in order) apostles, secondarily prophets, thirdly teachers, AFTER THAT" {meaning, after the foundation is laid). After the purpose of God were divinely established, the rest of the Gift Offices were added – ALL for the maturing of the saints for the work of the ministry.

A foundation is the undergirding upon which everything else rests. This foundation holds up the structure that will advance the Kingdom. The prophets should function in conjunction with – and be complementary to the grace of the apostolic that God gives the church.

The ministry Offices of the apostle and prophet are Gifts and callings, NOT a sign of spiritual attainment. There are qualifications to fulfill that Office, but God calls people by His grace and He chooses them by His grace, by His sovereignty, and according to His purposes and foreknowledge.

What makes today so powerful? The fact that together, *we "are complete (WHOLE, undivided, compete, inner-connected, and unified) in Him"* (Col. 2:10).

We understand the Gift Offices intersect and inter-relate. Diversity of Gifts is necessary and we must learn to function together to gain greater impact. Each Gift FUNCTIONS differently, with differing strengths. Together, they overlap to build Kingdom influence and effectiveness.

The Lord awakens us to new never before discovered realms of the Spirit. The Spirit insistently urges us to move past the religious and into the strength of combining the apostolic influence on the prophetic.

Old Testament Prophets seemed to function more like New Testament apostles.

GENERALLY SPEAKING, the apostle is *sent* to break through and establish new territories for the Kingdom of God, to inaugurate and clarify Biblical purpose and determine in new arenas to be conquered.

Apostolic leaders must have a profound prophetic and revelational ability. However, apostles *tend* to focus on vision, goals, solutions, defining doctrine, and building strategy. They tend to minister more out of principal, direction, and getting things done!

Apostles advance other ministries. They fuel us to push beyond known limits and to change the way things are.

In Creation, God SPOKE, "Let there be!" That's Prophetic and within those creative words is the *power* to produce.

Then He took dirt, formed it, and blew into it! That's Apostolic – the intention was ordered and completed.

To learn how to have an apostolic mindset and how apostles function here is a great Online School: http://www.kluane.com/index.php/reformation/theschooloftheapostles

New Testament Prophets

New Testament PROPHETS generally speak into an entity that is already in existence, while apostles tend to be the initiating pioneers who establish entities. Both functions are necessary and both can overlap in function and leadership.

A prophetic person will cooperate in that breakthrough by bringing fresh insight as well as the tireless sense of encouragement to the people.

The prophetic leaders look at that same vision and problem of the apostle. Their function is to detect the hidden. deliver a more extemporaneous and expression of the quickened Spirit of God. Prophecy reveals Christ and activates people to seek Him.

Of course, there are exceptions to these *generalities*.

"Among the prophets and teachers of the church at Antioch of Syria were Barnabas, Simeon (called "the black man"), Lucius (from Cyrene), Manaen (the childhood companion of King Herod Antipas), and Saul." (Acts 13:1-2).

This previous Scripture shows us that the great first-century church in Antioch was primarily led by prophets and teachers. There was no mention of apostles in *that* particular church. This shows us that present-day prophetic leaders can oversee and lead large organizations or networks.

Neither Gift Office can be confined to single characterizations or designations. They overlap and combine. An *apostolic* prophet is one who operates as a prophet from an apostolic world view. A prophetic apostle is one who functions as an apostle and who has a strong prophetic gift. (Each of the 5-fold Gift Offices can and should be prophetic, etc.)

 Prophetic words are the declaration of an invitation from the Lord to aggressively pursue and lay hold of Kingdom issues.

Prophecy is sometimes difficult to find definition because each person tends to hear differently. But, the reason, effort, and motivation in our pursuit of Gifts should be accomplished through Grace. Building a "good dream" rather than a "God dream" is simple. It is all to easy to birth an Ishmael rather than to birth the promised Isaac. We never want our own agenda rather than the Lord's.

Why would we want to view the prophetic from an apostolic lens?

The apostolic looks for the prophetic to not just be another utterance but a word in season to initiate decisive action.

1. The apostolic mindset is particularly focused on ORDER, SAFETY, and RELIABILITY. Right now, leaders need to bring proper caution to guard and protect the Church within proper limits and boundaries – while at the same time allowing a much greater release of the Spirit of God.

2. The apostolic influence upon the prophetic demands the emergence of greater revelation WITH ETERNAL IMPACT and CONSEQUENCE.

3. Prophetic gifts that align with apostolic vision can have ultimate influence. It is decisive and determined while projecting insight upon that vision and may bring strategic ideas for action as well as warnings about what is ahead.

4. The true prophetic should be marked with significant NOW words, critical insight, and key and crucial awareness and perceptiveness. The value is that the prophetic can keenly reach into the heavenlies to obtain precise revelation for the time we live.

5. The prophetic Gift must be consistently honed, refined, polished, improved, and sharpened.

6. An apostle must lead with prophetic influence.

> *No more fluff and superfluous words. No more merchandizing a Gift! IT'S TIME TO GAIN RESPECT BACK TO THE PROPHETIC!*

- What is our prophetic response to these times of great opportunities and what should we do next?

- What does Divine order look like? Sound like?

- How do we move into the next dimension? How do we do things right? How do we lead forward?

How do we call believers into their destiny and identity in God?

- HOW do we vitally communicate relevance of our message into this CHANGING NEW DAY?

- How does the prophetic community represent the Lord as a full grown SON and heir – and not just a messenger?

Ideally, the Church should be apostolically led and prophetically influenced. And, working gifts together will allow heaven to invade our earthly sphere with startlingly fresh understandings of God's truth and direction.

The Spirit of Prophecy

True prophecy reveals the heart of God and proclaims his affection for His people, and His jealous longing for us to end everything that separates us from His presence.

Jesus is the whole message. HE IS the final word from God." *You were enriched in everything by Him in all utterance and all knowledge, even AS THE TESTIMONY OF CHRIST WAS CONFIRMED IN YOU, so that you come short in no gift, eagerly waiting for the revelation of our Lord Jesus Christ"* (1 Cor. 1:4-7).

To repeat, the testimony of Christ comes to you. Revelation 19:10b says that the testimony of Jesus is the *spirit of prophecy*. We should long to be drawn closer to HIM. Prophecy is not to validate us personally, but to exalt Jesus.

The angel told John, "The testimony of Jesus is the SPIRIT OF PROPHECY" (Rev. 19:10 NKJV). The ultimate purpose of prophecy should be TO REVEAL WHO JESUS *IS*, what HE *DOES,* and how HE *FEELS.* This is the type of prophecy with which all believers can operate.

THE SPIRIT OF PROPHECY is neither Gift nor Office, but an ANOINTING (1 Chron. 25:1-3).

The "Spirit of Prophecy differs from the "Office of the Prophet." This anointing is present and available to every believer at corporate gatherings of Saints.

The "spirit of prophecy" can be activated by faith in the same way as you accept salvation or the Gift of the Holy Spirit. As always, prophecy speaks beyond your own thinking.

 The SPIRIT of PROPHECY is given to build-up the church, or call them nearer to god as a group, or speak intimately to the group as a whole.

Prophecy communicates in words a Divine impression, a vision, a Word of Wisdom, discernment, the Word of Knowledge, revelation, illumination, enlightenment, dream, or quickened thoughts, etc. for the benefit of everyone. These can all be expressed and verbalized in a prophetic manner.

If you have the Holy Spirit you have everything you need to encourage and build up the Body.

Everyone has Gifts resident within that need to be developed. Gifts can be enhanced, activated, trained and developed through proper mentoring (1 Ki. 19:15-21, 2 Ki. 2:1-15, Lk. 10: 1-11, 19, Heb. 5:14). Gifts can be acknowledged, confirmed, and/or enforced by the laying on of hands (Deut. 34:9, Acts 9:17-18, 1 Tim. 5:22).

For God talks to God! And He looks to connect with that God part of you.

Levels

An important thing to keep in mind concerning the gift of prophecy is that there are LEVELS OF PROPHECY.

1. There is a GENERAL level in which the saints of God are encouraged to be released in, which is basically for edification, comfort and exhortation.

All believers are told that they can prophesy in a general manner. However, being able to prophesy WELL does NOT necessarily mean that you are an actual 5-fold prophet.

THE SPIRIT OF PROPHECY (GENERAL) of the believer should NOT be concerned with foretelling or forth telling. This is the "Spirit of Prophecy" that is available to all. The Scripture is clear that "ALL may prophesy" (1 Cor. 14:31). So this gift is one that you should ask for, practice, and use. Being able to prophecy well does not necessarily make you a "prophet."

> Saul was activated and impacted when he was surrounded by the prophets, but he was not known as a prophet (1 Sam. 10:5-6).

We must all covet to prophesy (1 Cor. 14:39). "One by one that all may learn and all may be encouraged"(1 Cor. 14:31)!

2, THE LOCAL PROPHET: There is another level of prophecy that is reserved for those who are more experienced or recognized as "local prophets," which involves a higher level of insight.

3. THE OFFICE OF PROPHET deals with correction, national influence, divine foretelling, prediction, or forth telling (we'll talk more about that later).

4. Sometimes, when you are in the presence of strong prophetic gifts, the ability for you to prophesy could increase or become activated. A person can minister out of the unction of the presence of God or out of their Gift.

The Purposes Of Prophetic Gifts Are:

1. TO BUILD-UP THE BODY, to call people nearer to God, or speak intimately to them.

2. TO DECLARE GOD'S INTENTION to bring forth His nature and action in this world and upon others. God's purpose in the earth is the Kingdom. Jesus spoke about the Kingdom and Kingdom purpose.

They shall speak of the glory of Your kingdom and talk of Your power; to make known to the sons of men his mighty acts, and the glorious majesty of his kingdom. Your kingdom is an everlasting kingdom, and Your dominion endures throughout all generations (Ps. 145:10-11).

3. **TO IMPRINT OTHERS with a Divine sense of PURPOSE. The Kingdom is not in the distant future, it is here and NOW. This reality gives us purpose.**

4. **TO EXPAND THE SPIRIT AND TRANSFORM THE SOUL of those who receive and then boldly begin to live out God's plan on this earth.**

5. **TO MOTIVATE AND ACTIVATE others to become the living and breathing embodiment of Christ on earth. To speak dominion revelation that moves the saints of God into corporate destiny.**

When given correctly, everyone's Gift is amplified and becomes more meaningful through converging.

Chapter 2: Order

ORDER & PROTOCOL

Let all things be done decently and in order (I Cor. 14:40).

After studying the Great Revivals of the past, we discover the main reasons for their decline usually has to do with excesses. We believe that by providing safety standards and righteous cautionary boundaries, many excessive errors will be reduced and genuine moves of God can be extended.

Providing a solid environment for a Genuine Move from God will sustain it longer.

"We desire (long and have passion) to prophesy and must not despise (treat with contempt, have undervalue, do not treat lightly, or scoff) it" (1 Thes. 5:20).

At the same time that we welcome and pursue the best gifts, we are also commanded to use wisdom and discernment to avoid misuses.

Any order given should increase our desire to perfect this imperative Gift.

As we strive to speak and minister accurately for the Lord, we must also carefully consider the Word of God in order to give accuracy and strength to our assembly.

For me, there is nothing more important than representing the Lord with all integrity. My practice is that I don't say "GOD SAID" unless I'm totally certain of that as a fact. That's right... it's that imperative to me to hear correctly. I want people to be able to go to the bank with what was said to them – If it is just an impression, then it is conveyed as that.

Be cautious about repeatedly saying, "God told me" or "Thus saith the Lord" all the time! Over-familiarity and redundant phrases make us careless, or even proud. We tend to lose our reverence that these statements demand. Repetition can cause an under-evaluation of what these statements mean.

When you say, "God said," you should be ready to fight to defend that statement to the end.

Honor your words. It is an unfathomable honor to speak for the Lord.

The Apostolic View of Prophetic Focuses On Order.

Believe it or not, the church is not breathlessly waiting for your gift. Neither is the local pastor. It is imperative to learn to walk in humility and find the right doors - they are usually not where you expect or even desire.

A pastor (local church leader) often has a different temperament from a prophet. He/she has a heart for the local congregation and patiently shepherds and guards them daily. True prophets often have a wider or more global view.

PROTOCOL speaks of expectations. Knowing guidelines and protocol will show you how to FIT into what is expected! Then you can maximize yourself inside that expectation.

Order and protocol are never intended to limit prophecy – but to increase accuracy. Correct protocol enables us to effectively communicate HOW TO DO something correctly! It brings resolution and strategy to areas of tension and conflict.

> *PROTOCOL effectively communicates how to do something the right way.*

You and I have the GREATEST message in the world – one of redemptive Kingdom dominion. It tells how mortality is swallowed up by LIFE. As we enter into our true habitation in the Spirit (2 Cor. 5:1), the consummation comes and Christ is ALL in ALL. Now!

Correct order and protocol will help us greatly to properly communicate the profound Divine message into our human dimension of under-standing and comprehension.

Protocol for Services

Believers are told to *covet* to prophesy. *Covet* (NT:2205) means to eagerly desire earnestly, to have fervent heat, zeal, and ardor to *prophesy* (mean-ing to speak forth as an intermediary under Divine inspiration the mind and counsel of God). Prophecy is the voice and words of Christ speaking to His Body.

Unfortunately, there are many who have suffered from a misuse of some ministry gifts, and therefore this book is written to help leaders define their expectations and also to exhort the believer to cooperate with the agreed use of private and public ministry and especially regarding prophecy.

You should know that the expectations, protocol, and practice of prophetic ministry differs from place to place - and each assembly desires safety and accuracy for their congregation. Each place has developed procedures and expectations. You need to understand and respect these individual rules before you proceed!

You must learn to understand the differences between the governmental leadership of a local church and the role of revelatory gifting. Both are vital. Both must learn to mutually function, honor, cooperate, esteem one another. Both must learn to not compete.

Many problems and excesses develop when believers fail to comply with the boundaries of the local assembly. Cooperation must accompany your God given privileges. True prophecy and prophetic words must fall under the guidelines given in Scripture to govern the use of spiritual gifts (1 Cor. 12:4-11) and under the rules of that particular Church. Protocol is necessary in a local setting. Unless you are instructed otherwise by the leaders of that assembly, these guidelines should be your expectation.

All forms of government establish protocol which is the behavior and customs between ambassadors, kingdoms, governments, and military etc. Protocol is honorific. It is expected procedure, dress, how to address dignitaries, etc.

The local church should establish protocol of what they expect in terms of behavior and ORDER.

Guidelines are like a railway track to a train. Too many times, prophetic ministries get derailed and crash because of misuse or abuse of prophetic gifts. Guidelines and protocols help prevent these situations from occurring.

Local leaders want to know you and train you to excel in the Gifts so that you will understand how to function within their expectations!

In this urgent time, every local church and gathering as well as every meeting should have a clearly defined prophetic protocol.

 We need to release reliable and accurate gifts from confident ministers!

When you understand what the protocols are, you can experience freedom within the framework of guidelines.

The congregation benefits from the exercise of a loving, and safe prophetic ministry that brings great blessing to them and the church.

Prophecy and the delivery of Spiritual Gifts can have phenomenal life changing effects for the good or serious consequences, and even damage to precious lives. This should not be taken lightly. Please understand that any caution is for your safety and the safety of others.

Pertinent Prophetic Protocol

Leaders generally expect the general membership to operate in the Gifts of the Holy Spirit as differing from the Office of the prophet. To maintain ORDER and accuracy, only those with proven, assigned, and/or recognized prophetic ministry may correct, tear down, or give specific personal direction or correct placement, activation, and/or fitting.

 1. All believers are supposed to prophesy, that does not mean they are a prophet. It does not make you more spiritual than others. Every member is called to participate in God's prophetic plan – all can prophesy encouragement to the body. It does not mean you should be singled out.

2. Remember that you prophesy in PART. That means you can make mistakes. The best thing is to stand ready, willing, and even desirous of being corrected (1. Cor. 13:9).

3. Correction is not rejection. Prophetic gifts must be subject to and submitted to delegated local church authorities as well as those in authority at conventions, etc. It is up to you to comply with that expectation.

You only steward your Gifts. Think of yourself as a bank teller who has a million dollars pass through their hands. Don't take credit! It doesn't belong to you, Really, it doesn't. Don't take offense in correction, but allow it to lead you forward and learn to excel.

Rejection, persecution, and resistance is all part of learning and growing. Remember that Jesus did not open His mouth to defend Himself.

4. All gifts must come out of LOVE.

Prophetic ministry can be a powerful and effective Gift that when properly motivated can deliver specific strategies, secrets, and breakthrough concepts.

Important Reasons Why Guidelines and Protocols Are Needed:

"Wherefore, brethren, covet to prophesy..." (1 Cor. 14:39-40)

When you understand the importance of order, you will begin to excel in Biblical prophetic operations. We covet to prophesy in excellence.

The Bible says, "...Covet (desire greatly) to prophesy and forbid not to speak with tongues. Let all things be done decently and in *ORDER*" (1 Cor. 14:39-40). *Order* is the word *taxis* (where we get the word taxi) that means an "ordered flow."

Order creates necessary Scriptural boundaries that must accompany your God given privileges. True prophecy and prophetic words must fall under the guidelines given in Scripture to govern the use of Spiritual Gifts (1 Cor. 12:4-11).

As order is established within the local church so that the Holy Spirit can move freely and minister to the congregation "dividing to every person severally as He wills" diversities of gifts, administrations and operations (1 Cor. 12). When order is in place, amazing spiritual dynamics can release the empowerment of the Holy Spirit.

Guidelines and boundaries rightfully in place, build strong and safe Churches.

Therefore, spiritual cooperation with the ORDER (*taxis*) of the house always brings about spiritual protection that guards believers from being hurt and misguided while also releasing the Holy Spirit to move without hindrance.

One of many Biblical precedents for protocol is when the Apostle Paul gave clear guidelines for prophetic ministry to the Corinthian Church. He advised the church to put protocols into place for prophecy to operate in church meetings (1 Cor 14:26-33).

Protocol guidelines help provide a safe environment for church leaders, the prophetic people involved, and the congregation. Protocol therefore builds greater confidence in prophetic ministry.

Guidelines can be used when something unhealthy or potentially damaging occurs that needs to be addressed.

- For example, they can describe what actions to take when an unhealthy or potentially damaging event occurs (i.e. someone brings an "wrong" prophecy).

- Should a problem happen, guidelines provide a reference and guide for restoration, while enabling continuing freedom for the Gifts of God to operate in the church.

They provide a strong framework within which spiritual gifts can be released and operate freely with accountability.

They bring everyone 'on the same page,' (i.e. if a new person comes into the church who has prophetic gifts but has a differing perspective on their use, it gives them something so they can understand your expectations).

Protocol provides a means of guarding and teaching everyone (and in particular for this study the prophetic people and intercessors in the church).

Provide a track for training people who desire to operate and grow in prophetic ministry. If you are a person in the church who is gifted in prophecy or other revelatory gifts, then find out the local guidelines and adjust accordingly. These guidelines may change as the church changes and grows.

What Kinds of Prophetic Guidelines Should a Church Have?

Regarding personal prophecies (given from individuals to individuals within the church, protocols should be unique and individualized to a local church. This can be affected by a number of factors that may include:

- The unique vision and values of that local gathering.
- The size and prophetic experience of that congregation.
- The desired outcomes and goals for that assembly that you might not know about.
- The particular needs of that local Body.

Protection

Proper order protects the flock from being misled, false anointing, and familiarity. "Order" needs to be established. Beloved, as we build Kingdom communities, networks and ministries, be watchful. Understand that what you are building will be invaded by any and all of the following.

- False Prophets (Mt.7:15)

- False Witnesses (Mt.15:19)

- False Christ (Mt.24:24)

- False Apostles (2Cor.11:13)

- False Brethren (2Cor.11:26)

- False Teachers (2Peter 2:1)

- Strange Doctrine (Heb. 13:9)

- Another Gospel (2Cor. 11:4)

> *"Beware of false prophets which come to you in sheep's clothing but inwardly are ravening wolves. Ye shall know them by their fruits"*
> (Mat.7:15-16).

(*They are*) Speaking perverse or perverted things and distorting truth (Acts 20:30 NIV)

"Thus says the Lord of hosts: "Do not listen to the words of the prophets who prophesy to you. They make you worthless; They speak a vision of their own heart (they say things that people want to hear and they do their own thing, Jer. 23:16-22).

"The prophets prophesy lies in My name. I have not sent them, commanded them, nor spoken to them; they prophesy to you a false vision, divination, a worthless thing, and the deceit of their heart.... I did not send them" (Jer. 14:14).

FALSE PROPHETS want to draw/tear away disciples after themselves (NLT) in order to draw a following (Acts. 20:30).

They cause you to make mistakes by their lies (Jer. 23:32).

False prophecy does not come from a true prophet. It is deceptive, misleading, and/or creates idols. There is a counterfeit demonstration in some psychics, occult, New Age, and paranormal phenomenon.

Psychics can be very accurate -- but they function from the wrong source.

POOR PROPHECY can be a mixture of incorrect interpretation so that the message is distorted. Poor prophecy could be a harsh, or condemning, or directional, or correctional, or personal opinion. This is out of order in a public setting.

Weak prophecies say very little.

The "resident anointing" to prophesy comes from WITHIN New Testament believer (Col. 1:27, Eph. 3:17, Col. 3:16, Acts 2:4, 1 Jn. 2:27, John 14:17). That anointing is there to exalt Jesus alone... it's about revealing the LORD Who LIVES IN you.

THE NON-BELIEVER CAN BENEFIT FROM THE PROPHETIC

Prophecy also has purpose for the non believer (or uninformed). 1 Corinthians 14:23-25 tells us that by hearing prophecy, the non-believer can e:

Convicted of needing to engage with God or to confess.

Convinced with a realization of greater reality or truth.

Compelled with a desire to surrender.

PROPHETIC WORDS AFFECT BELIEVERS IN CERTAIN WAYS:

To be convinced: to go further, not give up, continue with a task. It will causes them to be "fully convinced that what God has promised He is well able to perform" (Rom. 4:21). To make ready.

To speak and hear acceptance and love: Out of love alone will Your words be that "certain sound" yielding truths rather than just sounding brass (1 Cor. 14).

To proclaim: Nehemiah 6:7 says that prophets (*nabiy*) proclaim (call out, herald, announce, tell).

To call to consecration: Until Aaron was consecrated; he could not stand as the prophet (Ex. 40:13).

A true prophetic word can prepare the hearer to fully experience the *zoe* LIFE that God (already) predestined for them (Ro.8:29). It declares a hidden and unseen nature and calls forth what is not as though it IS already. And it speaks forth that which is yet to come. (1 Jn. 3:1-3).

Good prophecy can be summed up to say, "This is who I'm longing to be in you, this is how I want to empower you, and this is how I want you to impact others."

Remember, there's a difference between a revelatory gifting for general personal ministry and that of a 5-fold gift of a Prophet.

The Prophetic

There are three major divisions in TYPES of the Prophetic.

1. THE GIFT OF GENERAL PROPHECY. This Gift is given to every believer.

2. THE MINISTRY OF THE PROPHETIC. Many people prophesy well and some are acknowledged as "prophets" in their local sphere, or local Church. Some of these may become future 5-fold Prophets.

3. 5-FOLD PROPHETS. The OFFICE of being a 5-fold prophet is DIFFERENT from the GIFT of prophecy or the Ministry of the Prophetic. Everyone can prophesy with the GIFT of prophecy, many prophesy well. BUT ONLY A FEW ARE 5-FOLD PROPHETS with global reach. One of the greatest problems in the church today is that we have not clearly defined this differentiation.

The Chart below attempts to show the DEPTHS of the PROPHETIC. We will break down these groups and look at some distinguishing parts.

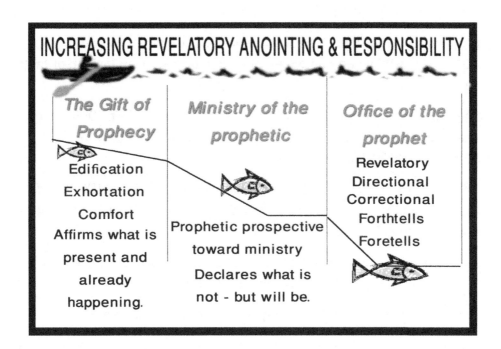

INCREASING REVELATORY ANOINTING & RESPONSIBILITY

The Gift of Prophecy	Ministry of the prophetic	Office of the prophet
Edification		Revelatory
Exhortation		Directional
Comfort		Correctional
Affirms what is present and already happening.	Prophetic prospective toward ministry Declares what is not - but will be.	Forthtells Foretells

GENERAL PROPHECY

"I am the Lord who has made all things.... who carries out the words of his servants and fulfills the predictions of his messengers..." (Is. 424-26).

Scripture tells you that ALL CAN PROPHESY... isn't that the most wonderful realization?

General prophecy is a spontaneous supernatural utterance in a KNOWN tongue.

Prophecy is a GIFT. We as believers have the *potential* to speak as the oracles of God (1 Pet. 4:11).

Prophecy can contribute and add to what you already know and contribute CONFIRMATION. It can add a plan of action, a maneuver, insight, or tactical idea.

The Greek word for prophecy means to "speak for another." Or in other words, TO BE A SPOKESMAN FOR GOD BY THE INSPIRATION OF THE SPIRIT AT THE MOMENT.

THROUGH THE PROPHETIC GIFT YOU CAN SPEAK SUPERNATURALLY TO PEOPLE and express the coming forth of spiritual culture, Divine realities, and of the Kingdom and heaven.

> *"The prophetic dimension is the audio-visual department of heaven."*
> Dr. Bruce Cook

Prophecy is the unction of the Holy Spirit and not of your soul.

Prophecy is the voice of the LORD upon the earth bringing His counsel. Prophecy is the declaration and release of God's powerful intention. (See stories about Elijah in 2 Kings, Amos 3:7).

In Matthew 10:27 Jesus said, *"The things I am whispering in your ear you proclaim them from the housetops."* Prophesy expresses the heart and mind of God.

But you don't have to say everything you hear. There were other times when Jesus told some people not to tell anyone, but to keep His secrets. We see therefore, that the true essence of the prophetic is to have intimate relationship with Jesus and know *when* to speak, how, and *where*.

Scripture says, "if any man speak, let him speak as the oracles (*logion* = fluent utterance, masterful, complete) of God" (1 Pet. 4:11).

Should Have Good Doctrine

 The revelation that you are capable of delivering is based on the level of comprehension of God's Word that you walk in. This expands what Paul said in Romans 12:6 that a person will *prophesy according to the proportion of faith given to him.*

 Everyone tends to minister and prophesy out of their own understanding and doctrine of Who God is. *You cannot prophesy beyond your doctrine.*

How are we ever to receive fresh revelation when we are supporting bad information?

Because of this understanding, you must continuously move forward with "PRESENT TRUTH," much like the cloud moved before the children of Israel (Is. 43:19). It is vital that you be continually expanding your revelation of Him.

The Lord God constantly reveals Himself in a new dimension – He is "ever revealing." He becomes what is needed at the point of need.

Static doctrine causes unfruitful ministry. Wrong doctrine can keep you from speaking out what you hear today – a word of change. Make sure that your studies keep you relevant and current.

Open your heart and allow the Lord to teach you – and reveal through you. Allow Him to change your theology and your mindset whenever necessary. An authentic word will perhaps give additional information concerning the present mission and intention of God.

That being said about progressive truth, it is equally imperative that you not break the solid boundaries of foundational Scripture. The properly translated Scripture is the ultimate trumpet of God's purposes and will. It is our plumb line. A prophetic community must take pains to be totally accurate.

YOUR WORDS MUST LINE UP WITH THE BIBLE. You need to read and know the Scriptures – you must become acquainted with the Word as a "Present Truth and Finished Work."

YOUR WORDS MUST BE RELEVANT AND CURRENT. This isn't just about reciting the facts and topics of the Bible – you should go deeper and understand the connotations and significances of the Word of God!

Jesus did not just "repeat the Word." He explained and unveiled the relevant significance and application.

YOUR WORDS MUST SPEAK TO THE SPIRIT. A "*confirming word*" speaks to the spiritual and does not appeal to the ego. It speaks to potential and will reinforce what the hearer already knows to be true. It doesn't speak to flesh, suspicion, or accusation. (It can cause the hearer to rise up and begin again.)

YOUR WORDS CAN DEMONSTRATE THE POWER OF GOD. Gifts of the Spirit affirm that God's actual presence leads us.

YOUR WORDS CAN CRY OUT FOR PERSONAL HOLINESS AND REPENTANCE. Prophecy never pets sin. But, it also never exposes private sins to the masses. Nor, does it move in judgemental ways against the choices and actions that you personally disagree with.

- Precise words can jolt someone out of complacency and awaken their heart with a personal desire for deeper revelation.

- Prophecy speaks under the influence of Divine inspiration in the common language of the speaker and hearers.

All believers can give General prophecy that brings EDIFICATION, EXHORTATION, AND COMFORT (Rom. 12:6, 1 Cor. 12:10).

But everyone who prophesies (speaks what God has revealed) speaks to people (as to be understood) for their exhortation (strengthening), encouragement (building up), and comfort (consolation) (1 Cor. 14:3).

You should FIRST learn to bring edification, exhortation, and comfort in every thing that you speak. You can investigate, excavate, find patterns, and illuminate what is happening. You can confirm and activate.

We could paraphrase this verse above to say, "Desire to earnestly hear God and speak in order to edify, exhort and console or give comfort to all men."

We de-mystify the prophetic when we understand that it is hearing and speaking what the Lord wants to communicate. After all, who does not want or need to be edified, exhorted and consoled, or comforted?

Many problems and excesses develop when people assume that they are exempt from this definition of how to share their impressions. Believers using their gifts should not bring condemnation, guilt, fear, or correction.

"Therefore encourage one another and build each other up, just as in fact you are doing" (1 Thes. 5:11).

"EDIFICATION" means to build up and strengthen and *"to build a house."* This type of prophetic word will build up the people and the house of God; it will encourage spiritual growth. To edify is to enlighten and inform. A well timed word of encouragement becomes a life saver and a hope builder. Applicable Scripture is edifying.

"EXHORTATION" means, *"to call near."* To exhort is to urge, to press, to entreat, or to urge someone strongly. It is an appeal to propel a person to action. The primary sense of the word is to excite, give strength, spirit or courage...to embolden, to cheer or advise. You have respect for their conditions never impose your personal ideas.

"COMFORT" means, *"to speak intimately along side"* – for example when someone is in the midst of a trial and the word of the Lord suddenly becomes very personal and as real to them as a hand upon their shoulder. It is encouragement! And it is solace, comfort, and soothing consolation during trial. These actions can also bring restoration. All believers can speak edification, exhortation, and comfort.

- General Prophecy always gives the listener something to hope for, work towards, or pray through.

- It is NOT directive, but always encouraging.

- Prophecy can be used in personal overcoming. "Timothy, according to the prophecies previously made concerning you, THAT BY THEM YOU MAY WAGE THE GOOD WARFARE" (1 Tim. 1:18),

- Your warfare is convincing yourself that this is a Word from the Lord and then applying the discipline needed to achieve it.

- There will probably be a *gap* between what is promised and the observable fulfillment. Faith is needed to sustain that vision during this gap time.

- General prophecy strengthens and confirms. Acts 15:32, Now Judas and Silas, themselves being prophets also, exhorted and strengthened (*episterizo*= confirmed).

- PROPHECY MAY INTERTWINE WITH INTERCESSION. Much of intercession is prophetic in nature. "But if they are prophets, and if the word of the LORD is with them, let them now make intercession to the LORD of hosts..." (Jer. 27:18).

- PROPHETIC INTERCESSISON can pick up the desire or burden of God's heart. They will be able to interpret what God intends.

- Prophecy can bring prosperity. "So the elders... PROSPERED through the PROPHESYING of Haggai (and) Zechariah..." (Ezra 6:14).

THE MINISTRY OF THE PROPHETIC

Going a little deeper are the "local prophets" who prophesy well in a local sphere.

> This is a grand gift. But, here is generally where there can be some problems. Because people are eager to share they sometimes forget the protocol of a local assembly.

For Now! (Until We Know You)

In the past, there has been much hurt to the Body in the area of the prophetic. Because God's people are precious and sometimes misled, leadership needs to guard and protect their flock until they are mature!

How do we do that? It takes time to know people. Scripture insists that leadership know their flock (that includes those who labor prophetically).

> *"Be thou diligent to know the state of thy flocks and look well to thy herds"* (Proverbs 27:23).

Scripture says, "And we beseech you, brethren, to KNOW THEM WHICH LABOR AMONG YOU and are over you in the Lord and admonish you" (1 Thes. 5:12). Notice that you must know those who labor and know those who lead!

We want to know you!

WE WANT TO KNOW YOU. Period! You may have been trained elsewhere... but, you need to know the local expectations and how they guard the House of God. You need to be recognized by the set-leader.

If an individual is not recognized as a prophetic voice to that particular congregation, it is not proper *order*.

Unfortunately, sometimes people are not who they seem to be. Many times, deception comes to attack the Body. And, leaders can only know you in time.

May the Holy Spirit give you wisdom and understanding of why boundaries need to be set and enforced for everybody's protection.

General Vs. Individual Words

 If you are a visitor, learn first to get acquainted with those in charge. Then, ADDRESS THE ENTIRE CHURCH AS ONE UNIT. A corporate word where everyone is included, may well be the strongest presentation possible. Overall, greater influence is often made when the general membership is ultimately built up and motivated to move together.

An ONTIME Word that applies to everyone can take the roof off!

Additionally, though correct personal prophecy is invaluable and most important, for most public occasions, speaking to everyone may be of overall GREATER VALUE in prophetic operation. Do not assume it is lesser to speak to everyone – this maintains the BIGGER PICTURE.

Consider the unlimited potential of the Church and awaken the presence of Christ! Light the way beyond mediocrity. Enliven the power of God's healing. The greatest impact is a global reach and mindset. How can we activate to make a difference?

Personal Prophecy

If you are new to this group and feel you have a PERSONAL WORD or "PUBLIC DIRECTIVE" word that does not fall into the category of GENERAL ministry, please submit it privately to the minister in charge, or on note paper given to an usher during the service.

It is best to NOT prophesy to individuals where you are not known (pardon the double negative, but you get the idea). If you do, you will often meet with barriers and rejection.

There is a difference between the kind of prophesying that is spoken over individuals and the kind that is spoken over entire congregations and the Church as a whole.

Some people are hyper-focused on PERSONAL PROPHECY and somehow think that they must posture and give personal prophecies in order to be valid or recognized.

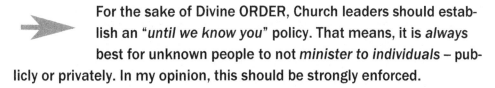 For the sake of Divine ORDER, Church leaders should establish an *"until we know you"* policy. That means, it is *always* best for unknown people to not *minister to individuals* – publicly or privately. In my opinion, this should be strongly enforced.

We've said it before: It is recommended that All PERSONAL prophetic individual ministry and directive words be delegated to those who have been approved by local church staff or those who are recognized to have already demonstrated a proven and legitimate ministry in a local area.

ONLY those with a proven and validated prophetic gift (or those with consent of the set-leader) are encouraged minister to an individual in public.

- If you have a "word" make sure that you have permission to give it.
- Leadership will let you know the time when it is appropriate to share. Please wait for that invitation.
- Those sharing in public ministry should first be recognized and receive permission to share.
- NEVER *assume* that it is okay for you to give a personal word to the meeting leader, unless they give you permission.

Leaders Must Make Prophetic Training Available.

THE 5-FOLD PROPHET

The office of a 5-fold Prophet is a governmental function. Some of them declare what God intends on grand levels of reach – city wide, state wide, nationally, globally.

The Lord shows them revelation.

They see problems and solutions.

They understand what is to be declared.

They declare the intention of God with authority and clarity.

They can take these insights and prophesy, preach, or declare them.

The Office of the Prophet is:

- Given by Jesus (Eph. 4).
- Given to some (Eph. 4:11, 1 Cor. 12:29).
- To give correction and direction.
- Given to lay foundations and equip. (Eph. 2:20, 4:12)
- Speaks of past, present, and future (Acts 11:28, 21:10-11).
- Speaks to nations (Acts 21:10, Jer. 1:5, 10).
- Becomes The Word (Agabus, Isaiah, Hosea).
- Makes God's desires known to the people.
- Speaks of Grace and judgment

Directive or future prophecy is best accomplished out of this Office.

- Recognized 5 fold prophets can corrective words or rebuke.
- They can tear down and build up.
- They bring correction.
- They speak to governments and nations on specific arenas.

- They may know specific information about identity, names, birthdays, financial problems, etc.

The words of Jesus are POWERFUL and SHARP (Heb. 4:12). They cut between the soul and the spirit and reveal the hidden purposes of the Lord.

Prophets come through the ranks of proving themselves. These people are the mouthpiece of God to His people. With the POWER of God in their declarations, they change the atmosphere of nations, governments, and world leaders. Their scope and reach are phenomenal.

Often, these people are set aside from before they were born (like Jeremiah). This Gift was imparted before the foundation of the world.

The 5-fold prophet is more seasoned and mature, established and recognized over time. He/she reveals truth that may be unknown to that point.

They ACTIVATE people to work and fulfill the mandated vision.

This Gift is distinctive. A 5-fold prophet can give correction and direction. They lay foundations and equip (Eph. 2:20, 4:12). They can speak of past, present, and future (Acts 11:28, 21:10-11).

They do not know everything about everyone all the time! But, they do make God's desires known to the people. They build foundations.

They speak of Grace and judgment. They attack unethical behavior, injustice, oppression, and barriers to what God wants to happen. They provoke the Church to hear and speak the "now" word about a "new thing" (Is. 43:18-19).

The "future word" speaks to the next phase of your future, while also giving meaning to your present as well. The *"new word"* tells you things that have never entered your mind, and you probably would never have considered (1 Cor. 2:9-10). It opens up new horizons and gives long term goals.

Prophecy can break cycles in finances and health. It can declare redemption and freedom, and challenge oppression. It can instruct on how God is moving NOW! It can bring repentance, conviction, instruction, and guidance.

Directive or directional prophesy is one of the most important aspects of the prophetic ministry. For example, in 1995, the Lord told me about a typhoon that was coming our way that would not be turned around. We had turned dozens away with prayer – but this one would be different.

Thankfully, everyone was able to prepare for this event. The winds were 236 MPH – and it was devastating. But, we were prepared.

And we cherish the fact that God speaks to us and warns us of things ahead. However, because of the frequent misuse and misunderstandings from this particular dimension of this gift, we have allotted this aspect of foretelling and direction to be used by the more mature in this gift. We want this to be accurate and SAFE.

THE KINDS OF PROPHECY

1. COUNTERFIET or soul realm prophecy. This may sound like the real deal, but the source is different. It can be out of the soul or out of the second heaven. When Jesus truly speaks through us, it is the testimony of Him. (Rev. 19:10).

Counterfeit words can come from soul realm ideas, Immature concepts. Familiar spirits. New Age influences. You must be sure to access the right source. Psychics do not access the right source. Flattery comes with all of these words to convince the hearer of untruth.

2. BUSINESS prophecy. Jesus told Peter to pay his taxes with a coin out of the mouth of a fish. The Lord can help you know what business to pursue. Marketplace spokesmen are ambassadors to the Kingdom.

> "And the elders of the Jews built, and they prospered through the prophesying of Haggai the prophet... and they finished it! (Ex. 6:14)

You should refrain from prophesying about business. But, practice on yourself and become proficient!

3. CULTURAL prophecy speaks to social groups, cities, and nations.

4. CORRECTIVE, DATED, and/or DIRECTIVE prophecy is generally for the most mature prophets to bring forth.

5. HEAVENLY prophecy speaks out of a third heaven. This is a spectacular experience of being "caught up" with the Lord. Secrets, mysteries, revelations, knowings.

6. CREATIVE prophecy speaks to the miraculous creation of something out of nothing. This kind of prophecy is uniquely not dependent upon the cooperation of people.

> Creativity speaks to ever part of God's creation and pulls it into completion and perfection.

There are no new revelations! Only light being shined upon that which was hidden. 'For with you is the fountain of life; in your light we see light" (Ps. 36:9).

The Lord calls people into that FINISHED PLACE. He stands at the finish line and prophetically calls them to come into their destiny.

The Old Testament Office Of Prophet

THE OLD TESTAMENT PROPHET *RECEIVED* revelation – whereas, the New Testament prophet *PERCEIVED* it. The Spirit "came upon" the OT prophets, while it flows "from within" those who are IN Christ.

As the prophets of the Old Testament wrote (or had scribes) their words were carefully guarded and kept. This later became books of our Holy Bible today.

Old Testament, prophets were mainly called to minister in a single geographic location because God was building the nation of Israel.

Sometimes, Prophets do prophetic acts to demonstrate what God is trying to do. (Isiah walked around naked. Hosea married a known prostitute. Noah built an arc.)

This Office often speaks what will later happen (Agabus, Isaiah, and Hosea).

Prophets can function in cooperating teams with the leadership who are assigned to build the house of God (Ezra, Nehemaih, Haggai). They help build by working in relationship to accomplish a unified goal. They spoke to social, political, economic, and geographical arenas (Nahum, Hosea, Obadiah, Elijah, Daniel, Agabus).

Apostles & New Testament 5-fold Prophets

The Greek word for "Prophet" is *prophetes* which means, "a foreteller and an inspired speaker of God." This Office is given by Jesus Himself. They are called to a specific group of people.

The early church appointed prophets who were SET (appointed to exhibit) in position as 5-fold prophets (1 Cor. 4:9). That is, these were separate from the Body who prophesied.

As with the apostle, the 5-Fold Prophet serves as a foundation gift for all other ministry gifts and for the Body of Christ (Ephesians 2).

Sometimes, it is very hard to tell the difference between a New Testament apostle and prophet because these Gifts can overlap.

In my opinion, a Prophet who is a woman, should be called a, "Prophet" and not "Prophetess."

They are usually endowed with the gift of exhortation and therefore often a revelatory preacher.

>> An apostle generally speaks from principle while a prophet speaks from the heart of God.

Prophets can be intense and insightful visionary leaders. They often have revelation of the condition of the Church and what God is doing in the future regarding the church and culture in their region or sphere of authority.

Prophets usually move in the Discerning of Spirits (determining truth and what is of God), and advanced interpretation of tongues.

Prophets have an extreme sense of right and wrong.

They are often introverts and prefer to be alone and solitary with very little social life.

Nabi

Most church leaders and traveling ministers who prophesy are what is called *nabi – (Nabih)* which is the Hebrew word meaning to bubble forth like a fountain – meaning that the Word of the Lord is effervescing up inside of you (like fire), and to pour forth words. This often means that a person can begin to prophesy at will. In other words, to be a spokesman for God by the inspiration of the Spirit at the moment.

The word "nabi" (*naba* and *nawbaw}* means to sing forth by inspiration expressing the eternal purposes of God.

"The Lion has roared, who shall fear? The Lord God has spoken, who can but prophesy (nabi)?" (Amos 3:8).

The *nabi* gift emphasizes declaring the ongoing words of God. It comes in a flash without forethought. Through this gift you can speak supernaturally to people and also to God. Nehemiah 6:7 says that prophets (*nabi*) proclaim (call out, herald, announce, and tell).

"And the Lord said to Moses, 'See, I have made thee a god to Pharaoh, and Aaron your brother shall be your prophet (nabi)" (Ex. 7:1).

"Oh, that all the Lord's people were prophets (nabi) and that the Lord would put His Spirit upon them" (Num. 11:29).

Nabi functioned in the authority of the Lord God to speak in His behalf.

Seers

"Believe God's prophet and so shall you prosper" (2 Chron. 20:20).

In the Old Testament, when men wanted to hear from the Lord, they went to a seer. *(Before time in Israel, when a man went to enquire of God, thus he spake, Come, and let us go to the seer: for he that is now called a Prophet was before time called a Seer)" (1 Sam. 9:9).*

Nine Old Testament men were called "seers" (*roeh, or ra'ah*) – meaning they see open visions and interpret them prophetically. Jeremiah was a SEER (*roeh*). Jesus often operated as a seer (Jn. 1:48, Lk. 10:18). (Also the Hebrew words *hozeh* and *Chazah* means seer.)

The word "hose" (*hozeh*) is used 22 times in the Old Testament and 11 of these times is used in connection with their name.

Seers mentally perceive, have vision, and prophesy from seeing. Their gifts may overlap with the use of Visions, "Words of Wisdom," etc.

The prophet Isaiah was told to write down in a tablet what the Lord said that it be a record forever. At that time, Israel would not hear (Is. 30:8-10).

"Let the Lord testify against Israel and against Judah by all the prophets and by all the <u>seers</u> saying turn ye from your evil ways and keep My commandments and my statutes. According to all the law in which I commanded your fathers and which I sent to you by my servants the prophets" (2 Kings 17:13).

David escaped into a stronghold of KIng Moab and the "...prophet (*hozeh*) Gad said, 'don't stay here in the stronghold; leave and go to Judah.' Then David departed and went into the forest of Hareth" (1 Sam. 22:5).

Here we see that Gad gave tactical instructions that David heeded. "Get out of here and get to a place of praise!"

"For when David was up in the morning the word of the Lord came under the prophet (hozeh) Gad which was David's <u>seer</u> saying,"-v1,"Go speak to David..." (2 Sam. 24:11).

Old Testament seers functioned under authority of a king. Heman spoke about the visions of Iddo, who was the seer to the wicked King Jeroboam (2 Chron. 12:15, 19:2). Jehu is shown to be a seer to King Jehoshaphat. Jeduthun is shown to be a seer to King Ahab (2 Chron. 25:15).

ROEH – Samuel was a *roeh* prophet who trained other prophets. He was regarded above the other seers of the day. *"Now the LORD had told Samuel in his ear a day before Saul came, saying......"* (vs. 15). The phrase "in his ear" literally means that God uncovered his ears!

Daniel was a (*roeh*) seer.

> Prophecy can speak prosperity. Ezra 6:14, *So the elders of the Jews built, and they prospered through the prophesying of Haggai the prophet and Zechariah the son of Iddo. And they built and finished it, according to the commandment of the God of Israel...*

Prosperity happened when they ACTED upon the word given to them.

Seers can function in PROPHETIC ministry and they can prophesy with instruments and as minstrels. They also have accountability structure, (2 Chron. 35:15).

Isaiah spoke of false "roeh" (29:10), "For the LORD has poured out on you the spirit of deep sleep, and has CLOSED YOUR EYES, namely, the prophets (chozeh): and he has covered your heads, namely, the seers (roeh)." (Notice that false prophets have closed or Fallen Eyes.)

Some seer prophets were also called the chozeh – or those particular seers who had deep understanding or spiritual apprehension of a truth.

The Watchman

The Hebrew word for prophecy is *dabar*, and that means "to drive forward what is behind." Inside a prophetic word is the power to bring that into being. Prophets are watchmen and forerunners.

Watchmen are positioned in a place to see and to warn. They tell what they see to those who need to hear it. A watchman tells what he/she sees (Is. 21:6).

"Set up the standard on the walls of Babylon; make the guard strong, set up the watchmen, prepare the ambushes, for the Lord has both devised and done what He spoke... (Jer. 51:12).

Watchmen see danger and whatever else is ahead.

"Son of man, I have made you a watchman for the house of Israel; therefore, hear a word from my mouth, and give them warning from me" (Ez. 33:6).

Watchmen are accountable and they MUST tell and warn of what they see.

"But if the watchman sees the sword coming and does not blow the trumpet, and the people are not warned, and the sword comes and takes any person from among them, he is taken away in his iniquity, but his blood I will require at the watchman's hand."

This is also the ministry of the Gatekeeper or Porter. The strong city gates were open and shut by the porter (2 Chron. 35:15). He was a guard over intruders. He set off an alarm if the city were invaded.

Learning HOW

"We have also a more (larger, greater) sure (stable, steadfast, forceful) word of prophecy (2 Pet. 1:19).

The Lord absolutely desires to speak to you. This Truth is at the heart of being able to participate in the Gifts of the Spirit. You must be convinced that God not only speaks today, but that He will actually SPEAK TO YOU. This extraordinary reality awakens hope and excites our faith to pursue prophecy confidently.

A person who ministers publicly should be a born again believer who has experienced the Baptism of the Holy Spirit and SPEAKS IN TONGUES. I believe that this is the *only* "door way" to accurate spiritual gifts. PERIOD. No exceptions.

The first stage after this is that you will receive some sort of impetus to begin – a receptivity from God in a vision, such as: revelation, impression, illumination, enlightenment, a mental picture, dream, or quickened thought (words) for the BENEFIT OF EVERYONE. Or, it could come as an inspired song. Also a Word of Wisdom, Discernment, or Word of Knowledge can be expressed in a prophetic manner. Always, this is beyond your own thinking.

The way that you receive your input will depend upon the unique way that God deals with you... each one of us is dealt with differently and none of us think or react in the same way. Some people receive very dynamic input while others move with suggestion.

The problem usually comes from how you choose to interpret this input. You must determine how that revelation concerns this particular event. (That is why you want to keep yourselves in holiness.)

After you get this impression, you can then begin to speak the APPLICATION of this information – that's prophecy.

Remember, prophecy is interpreted and communicated BY US!!! That's why we have to covet and desire to learn how to do it!!!

It is important to learn how to communicate what you believe God is telling you. You need wisdom to administer your words. You must filter out what needs to be said and what needs to remain quiet. What do the people need to hear? Should it be given publicly or privately?

Graham Cooke says that many charismatics think that prophecy should be "an empty thought passing through an empty head!" But, you must NOT kiss your brains good-bye! Be aware that your MIND is what you USE to bring forth a Godly word.

It is always appropriate to preface what you have to say with something like, "I have a strong sense that you....." Or, "I 'feel' that you will find great success in considering this...." "Is it all right if I share it with you?"

> *"Man's most noble efforts to serve God are laced with selfish intentions."*
> Martin Luther

The dividing line is that some ministries try to accomplish things 'for' or 'by' God – which is the great definition of "religion." However, it certainly is not necessary to DO WORK FOR God. This motivation of "TRYING to hard" tends to cause the greatest errors in the prophetic because that effort originates from personal ambition and can never accomplish what God longs to do 'IN,' 'through,' and 'with' us.

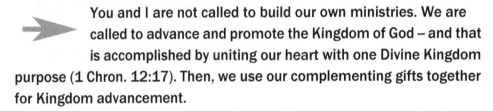 You and I are not called to build our own ministries. We are called to advance and promote the Kingdom of God – and that is accomplished by uniting our heart with one Divine Kingdom purpose (1 Chron. 12:17). Then, we use our complementing gifts together for Kingdom advancement.

- Gifts come together for unified purpose.
- Unite your heart with others. for the greatest impact.

You can have a significant "Call of God" on your life and miss it because of trying to make things happen from your unredeemed soul.

Another hindrance could be media. If you listen to the news and TV all day you will not have the sharpness to hear God. People often ignore the best opportunities to hear from Him through a preparation of silence, meditation, prayer, or reading the Word.

And most importantly, don't prophecy the bad news you hear. Don't empower the negative. If your words really have the power of life and death, then don't agree with the adversary. Call what is not as though it is! Speak the opposite of disaster. Speak the will of God.

And another thing, don't be fooled by the anointing that may be in the room. The crowds may be excited, the cheering and affirmation may be huge... and you can still be producing meaningless flesh. This is an imperative factor for learning how to properly access and activate the Gifts of the Spirit and to have right discernment.

Love is THE Fundamental Component of Prophecy

God's Love Must Become The Center Of Every Prophetic Word

The Lord is speaking right now, do you hear Him? Love is the preeminent expression of God.

It's not enough to merely "seek the mind of God," you must have the revelation of His HEART. Without love, the Apostle Paul says, we are nothing, and our words have an empty ring to them. You can prophesy, understand mysteries, and have great knowledge and it is nothing without love (1 Cor 13:1-3).

LOVE is always the "MORE EXCELLENT WAY" in using the gifts (1 Cor. 12:31). Earnestly desire the best gifts but *always* express them in love!

Love is the mode and method that surpasses all others.

"EVERYTHING you do must be done with love" (1 Cor. 16:14 NKJ).

if you have experienced the love of God and are filled up with that love, you will automatically want to share this love with others. Soon, all you want to do is encourage, uplift, and exhort them.

You must always remember that understanding God's LOVE is the center of being able to HEAR from Him.

If we have not experienced God's love for ourselves personally, we will be unable to express His love towards others.

Being aware of His love and mercy towards yourself in your own humanity and weakness enables you to communicate His love to others.

Most people are afraid to speak the Word of the Lord in fear that they will make a mistake. This is not the time to be concerned only about yourself. Just focus on loving and blessing – love is the only KEY! And you will NEVER be wrong.

Memorize this verse: "*The ONLY THING that counts is faith expressing itself through love*" (Gal 5:6).

LOVE must be etched upon every word spoken. "*If I have the gift of PROPHECY and can fathom all mysteries and all knowledge, and if I have a faith that can move mountains, BUT HAVE NOT LOVE, I am nothing*" (1 Cor 13:2).

Prophecies will fail, but love will remain (1 Cor. 13:8, 13).

Prophecy LOVINGLY communicates the intention and purpose of God.

But it's not enough to merely "seek the mind of God," we must have the revelation of His heart.

Love is the prerequisite to prophesy in any situation.

1. *Accurate prophetic ministry looks beyond what is seen outwardly in the natural*. God sees the inner heart of a person and speaks to the potential within.

Remember how God instructed Samuel as he sent him out to anoint the next King of Israel, "*Do not consider his appearance… People look at the outward appearance, but the LORD looks at the heart*" (1 Sam 16:7).

2. Love surpasses knowledge (Eph. 4:10). We do not base our prophetic words on what we know, or think. God's love supersedes our knowledge, our ideas, and our opinions.

Allow the Holy Spirit to deal with your set predeterminations and judgmental attitudes. Your preconceived opinions can actually obstruct your ability to see and hear. The unconditional LOVE of God must surmount all that you know.

3. Expressing God's Love in prophecy does not come from your natural emotions. The WAY you express your prophetic insight must be through the lens of God's Love. Jesus came to earth to die because of God's LOVE (Jn. 3:16).

True prophetic insight must be based from the ability to see people in their finished place. See where the Lord wants to take them. See them at their appointed destiny and call that forth. Always speak from this perspective and express God's unwavering love and acceptance.

'Follow the way of LOVE and eagerly desire spiritual gifts, ESPECIALLY the gift of prophecy.' (1 Cor 14:1)

Another translations says. *"Pursue love and desire (zello = be zealous) spiritual gifts, but especially that you may prophesy..."*

LOVE should guide the whole process of prophecy.

The WAY you deliver a Word should always be in LOVE. Be sure that the message you share is encouraging and empowering (1 Cor 14:3).

4. Love is Accountable. *"Eagerly pursue and seek to acquire love. Make LOVE your aim, your great quest..."* 1 Cor. 14:1 (Amp)

5. LOVE Covers and Does Not Condemn. It is not your job to uncover sin. You do not have to "rebuke" someone. God gives you and me the ability to let people off the hook an allow forgiveness to come. Just cut them some slack. Your assignment is to give them hope and a future!

1 Peter 4:8 *"Most IMPORTANT OF ALL continue to show deep love for each other, for love covers a multitude of sins."* What does that mean? Simply that LOVE COVERS a multitude of sins.

What is imperative is to KNOW that operating through LOVE will put that person's needs above your own opinions (Phil 2:1-8).

6. Prophetically ministering out of LOVE means that you bring HOPE to the hopeless. You speak what is not as though it is. You must not bring disappointment.

"Now hope does not disappoint, because the love of God has been poured out in our hearts by the Holy Spirit Who was given to us all (Rom. 5;5).

"These three things CONTINUE FOREVER. Faith, hope and love. And the greatest of these is love." Everything else you do and say can be temporary. But LOVE moves every single action into eternity and it becomes a legacy to last.

"Love the Lord your God with all your heart, soul, and mind. 'This is the first and greatest commandment. The SECOND MOST IMPORTANT is similar (as the first, important): 'Love your neighbor as much as you love yourself" (Matt. 22:36-39 LB).

"Greater love has no one than this: to lay down one's life for one's friends" (Jn. 15:13)

"Whoever does not love does not know God, because God is love" (1 Jn. 4:8 NIV).

"If we say we love God, but hate others, we are liars. For we cannot love God, whom we have not seen, if we do not love others, whom we have seen" (1 John 4:20, TEV).

"Love is more important than anything else. It is what TIES EVERYTHING COMPLETELY TOGETHER"(Col. 3:14, CEV).

*"Three things WILL CONTINUE FOREVER: faith, hope, and love. And the greatest of these is love."*1 Cor. 13:13 (NCV)

"No matter what I say, what I believe, and what I do, I'm bankrupt without love" (1 Cor. 13:3, MSG).

"Most important of all, continue to show deep love, FOR LOVE COVERS A MULTITUDE OF SINS" (1 Pet. 4:8, NLT).

"God WIPED OUT the charges that were against us for disobeying the Law... He took them away and nailed them to the cross" (Col. 2:14, CEV).

Apostles may be direct and strategic – but actions must come in LOVE.

When you speak out of His love, lives will change forever. These prophetic words give birth to the purposes of God.

Grace

With an enveloped and unveiled face you enter into His likeness and Who He is. You must always speak through grace to express the love of God.

 Grace is more than "unmerited favor." Grace is the power of God that enables you to accomplish your destiny!

His Grace empowers and brings comfort. Grace explains things you can't understand. Grace opens peace where there has been no peace. Grace tempers you and gives you understanding and compassion beyond your knowing. Allow Grace to carry your prophecies with Love.

Grace protects you from hurt and pain. It provides you with hope and strategy for tomorrow. Grace causes you to reach out. It stabilizes and brings rest. It brings confirmation, security, and awareness of His presence. It brings rest to your mind and restoration.

Remember that you are loved because of God's grace, and not because of your performance. His mercy reaches out to you continually as you grow.

"For I declare unto you," says the Lord, "that the release of this new day will arise within you that you may declare the glory of My habitation."

THE PURPOSE OF THE SPIRIT OF PROPHECY

Words have POWER. The literal translation of Luke 1:37 says, "For with God no word spoken by Him is without POWER." When we speak His Word, we release power. Elijah said, "As the LORD God of Israel lives, before whom I stand (relationship), there shall not be dew nor rain these years, except at my word" (1 Kgs 17:1). And that's what happened! (See also Is. 55:11, Jer. 1:12.). We're talking about the *real* kind of power that changes destiny.

The ultimate purpose of all prophecy and the communication of Spiritual Gifts should reveal who Jesus is, what He does, and how He feels (Rev. 19:10). Who does He want to be in you? How does He express Himself through you?

The Holy Spirit illuminates your heart (SOUL) and reveals truth. He then teaches you how to translate and communicate that into LIFE for others. You chase the One Who has drawn you. His heart responds to your cravings as He whispers unspeakable words and marvelously progressive unfoldings.

Christ IN you AND THROUGH you demonstrates the spiritual Gifts.

We long with holy passion to be a Spirit-filled people who participate in a prophetic Church and who present Jesus Christ as the only true hope for our world.

To do this demands that we be sensitive to the heart of God, and that we desire to reveal integral Divine purposes. Habakkuk 1:1 speaks of the *burden* of the Lord– this burden implies the heartfelt issues at stake, not just conceptual truths.

As the precious Holy Spirit actively falls in our midst, among our fallible flesh and blood, we see that God desires to impart to us. He uses us as vessels of His mercy - in spite of our shortcomings. With our human fallible in mind, we also know that the church is to be the prophetic servant in a multidimensional way.

We are the believers of God who are full of the Holy Spirit, desiring spiritual gifts and coveting to prophesy (1 Cor. 12:39). For this reason, we openly encourage everyone to present spiritual gifts to the body.

HEARING

There's a witness in your human spirit – something inside keys into the moment.

When God breathed into that lump of clay, Adam became a LIVING BEING. Like with Adam, the LORD wants to put His mouth upon us and breath INTO us the fresh and quickened breath of His Spirit.

That's what this prophetic life is all about... hearing Him breathe once again—and then exhaling the breath of God back to others.

We hear His voice in our garden heart. We hear Him in the wind. We discern His footsteps as He walks beside us in the cool of the day. He breathes new themes and reveals mysteries into our understanding. It's not just an old story, but one that revives our soul.

With His breath blown into us, we become a transporter of God's presence, a carrier of His intentions. To do that, we must use our words that will articulate the "now" Word. With prophetic words, we can speak the clear sounds of the trumpet and interpret the wind in the trees.

This prophetic generation must use words to awaken the church into a passionate and consecrated position. We carry the Word of the Lord, in the name of the Lord. We speak of a coming revolution of intimacy –

we hear His heart pounding against our ears. We hear His breath as he inhales and exhales. He fills our being with reverential awe.

Prophecy is the voice and words of Christ speaking inspiration to the church. From a New Testament lens, we become the mouthpiece of the Lord. With all of our being we desire to hear and speak forth those clear words from the throne that bring specific insights and strategies.

We bring a message that is ethical, vibrant, and relevant. We have the task of plowing up new territories that cannot be cultivated until we speak.

We are the messengers who carry words for others to hear. We determine that we will be encouraged in this journey to learn how to prophesy — and we purpose to give away what we have learned to those who are coming along behind us.

God gives us insight and hints. He does give us direction. We prophesy LIFE to dry places, to dry people, and to dry countries. Then, we have to walk by faith. Once we hear or give a prophetic word it is up to us to walk it out. It won't just happen without our cooperation. As we continue, suddenly the overall goal clarifies.

GOD STILL SPEAKS!

Learn how the Lord speaks to you and gives impressions.

"And the Lord came down in a cloud, and spoke unto him {Moses}, and took of the spirit that was upon him, and gave it unto the seventy elders: And it came to pass, that, when the spirit rested upon them, they prophesied and did not cease" (Num. 11:25).

Moses said, *"I WISH THAT ALL the Lord's people were prophets and that the Lord would put his spirit upon them ALL"* (Num. 11:29).

The Lord speaks differently to individuals (we discuss this in more detail later in this book). He speaks in your language and with your familiar expressions. Sometimes, He speaks directly.

"Not so with My servant Moses;... I speak with him face to face, plainly and not in dark sayings, And he sees the form of the LORD" (Num. 12:8).

"Your ears shall hear a word behind you, Saying... "(Is. 30:21). In Jeremiah 32:6, *"The word of the LORD came to Me saying... And then I knew that this was the Word of the Lord"* (Jer. 32:6). *"The word of the LORD came to Me saying... "(r. 3:6).*

"And then I knew that this was the Word of the Lord." Jeremiah heard the word, received it, believed it, and carried it out. We do not have to understand everything to DO IT.

There is balance in proper application: "Do not put out the Spirit's fire; do not treat prophecies with contempt. Test everything. Hold on to the good" (1 Thes. 5:19-21).

NOW

Discerning the voice of the Holy Spirit and communicating God's insights is not that hard. Learning to better discern the voice of the Spirit will enable you to make right decisions even during difficult situations. Scripture declares, "For as many as are led by the Spirit of God they are the sons of God" (Romans 8:14).

The Holy Spirit guides you to grasp Biblical principles and make right choices for your life, family, and ministry.

IT IS TIME TO BE RELEASED! The Greatest Breakthrough is simply in your MOUTH! Move out and begin. Get up and speak audibly and openly the Word of God. We need what you have. RISE UP with in the Word the Lord!

TRUTH: God wants to talk to you. He longs to impart His plans to you. Everyone who is filled with the Spirit of God can and should prophesy.

Unfortunately sometimes, hearing accurately from the Lord's Spirit seems difficult because there are many voices and distractions in the world.

There are many mystical misconceptions that keep the believer from understanding how to hear the Voice of the Lord.

My declaration for you dear reader is that you will awaken to hear the Holy Spirit speak to you afresh – and you will hear the voice of a loving God who LOVES this world unconditionally. You don't have to struggle anymore hearing from God. He speaks to you to encourage you to overcome fear and get started. Believers are His couriers of Good News.

* * *

As we pursue the best gifts, we are also aware that we are commanded to use wisdom and discernment to avoid misuses in the Gifts of the Spirit.

We want to HIT THE TARGET with accuracy, precision, and exactness. We purpose to make every effort to speak and minister precisely and truthfully for the Lord in order to bring strength to our assembly.

The church should allow much freedom in the administration of learning about the Gifts of the Spirit. Most of you reading this book desire to be activated into greater spiritual dimensions.

 Not only do you want to hear the Lord, but you need to communicate what you hear correctly! Not just speaking His Word out – but delivering it strategically so that it is understood and able to be followed.

CONTINUING FORWARD

I'm setting you up as a light for the nations so that my salvation becomes global! You'll proclaim salvation to the four winds and seven seas!
(Is. 49:6, Acts 13:47 MSG)

A person who prophesies must be a born again believer who has experienced the Baptism of the Holy Spirit and speaks in tongues. This is the <u>only</u> "door way" to all other spiritual gifts. Practice speaking in tongues – and then from that same "pathway" begin to prophesy.

Examine yourself honestly. The human element plays an important role in prophecy (1 Cor. 14:29-33). Learn to speak as an oracle of God, and not from your own thoughts being presented as a "word from God."

Be sure to bring a fresh word, not a repetition of empty exhortations you've heard on a recording or another service. Get a word that comes from the throne.

Be Christ-centered and not self-centered. Study, pray, and prepare your character. Do what is needed for the word to be accepted. Learn how to deliver words with love and authority.

Jeremiah 7:2b, ...*Hear the word of the LORD, all you of Judah who enter in at these gates to worship...*

Believe that you speak your word for God's highest and best to come forth. Speak with authority and allow your words to be released. You are a co-creator with God - the very One Who spoke the world into existence.

Rightly perceived and delivered prophecy can speak to the intangible Spirit realm and then form tangible expression within the world. You express the Divine infinite purposes of the Lord into reality.

A truly inspired word expresses God's thoughts through a human voice or action so that total salvation will be activated and embraced.

- Generally, it's best to not practice the first time on Sunday morning; give yourself time to learn. Before speaking to the whole assembly, try practicing in small meetings and teaching sessions where leaders can encourage you.

- Study pray, and make your life holy. Hear the voice of Jesus (Jn. 10:27).

- Rid yourself of the fear of man, the fear of rejection, confusion, frustration, anger, and bitterness.

- Your identity is not in what others say about you - it is in who God says you are. Rid yourself of the fear of man and the fear of the rejection of others. Apprehension brings confusion, frustration, anger, and bitterness. You must be emotionally healed in order to deliver a consistent and applicable word.

- Recording prophetic messages allows accountability when you begin. Be ready to learn to excel! Build credibility.

- Legitimate messages will consistently say what God says, not what you want Him to say. Don't twist words to fit your way.

- Minister without pride or doubt. Elitism and arrogance are not acceptable. Remember that you're loved because of God's grace, and not because of your performance.

- You probably won't know what you're going to say when you start, so don't analyze each word, but let it flow.

- Be humble. Humility is the absence of self-preoccupation and ministers without pride or doubt.

- Obey God's voice. Hearing God is one thing, doing what He says is another. (See story about Ananias who had clear instructions them. Also see Prov. 29:25)

- Be positive. Don't have a grudge or speak from anger.

- Super-spirituality limits your effectiveness. Be natural.

- Speak clearly – don't mumble or whisper.

- Don't scream or yell... God is not deaf.

- Don't talk too fast – it's hard to understand.

- Don't ramble on and on — people lose interest.

- Don't repeat yourself or someone who just prophesied before you.

- Give a word that harmonizes with what is happening at that moment. Get in the flow.

- Be encouraging. Don't condemn.

- Keep it simple and not mystical. Be real rather than phoney spiritual.

- Stick to a point. Be direct.

- Don't control a meeting that isn't yours.

- Be willing to be corrected.

DEFER TO OTHERS. In a public meeting, it is usually best to allow the more experienced people speak first – especially if you are just learning.

Everybody (including even the most experienced) should be accountable to the person in charge of the meeting. It is a blessing to cooperate with the authority that God places within an assembly.

Where ever you are, be safe. 1 Cor. 14:29 tells us to submit our messages for evaluation and discernment. That's why it is best for a local church to require that all prophetic ministries be given in public on a microphone, to be taped and evaluated. Accountability produces excellence. Be ready to learn to excel!

Do what is needed for the Word that you have to be heard and received. Purify your character so that the truth will not be rejected because of exterior mis-leadings.

"I Desire To Impart" (Rom. 1:11)

"For you have not passed this way before" (Josh. 3:4).

Even when I was a young Christian, and in a Spirit-filled Church, we were not allowed to freely discover how to engage with the Spirit of God beyond speaking in tongues.

Trying to keep order, the ancient Church Fathers made certain that they were the only ones who could speak for God. They limited the voice of the people and restricted the use of the Holy Spirit. Soon, the Dark Ages began and much truth was lost.

Today, we have a fresh wind upon us. The Lord God brings fresh impartation of His Spirit. Finally, mentoring leaders are arising to instruct the believer on how to accurately move in the Gifts.

BONES: When Elisha (the prophet who received the double portion) died, his bones were in left in a sepulcher. Another dead man was lowered onto Elisha's dead bones and the second man was revived (2 King. 13:21). There was an IMPARTATION OF LIFE.

Impartation refreshes and renews. The death and resurrection of Jesus causes you and me to have the opportunity to be activated so that the prophetic stream can be released. Begin now to proclaim and declare that you will begin to move in greater boldness in the area of prophecy.

Allow the impartation of the SPIRIT OF PROPHECY that brought life out of dead bones to activate and resurrect you!

IMPARTING: For the oil poured on the head must flow to the beard and then pour down and out to the rest of the body (Ps. 133:1-3). The oil (anointing) must flow TO the Body.

We see the apostles Peter and James say to the beggar, "Silver and Gold have I none, but such as I have I give." What was it that they had to give? No money. But, they had the weight of the Gifts of God within.

Ask yourself, what is in me? What do I carry to give? Without Jesus, you and I are nothing. But, with Him, others can rise up and walk at hearing *your words and mine.*

Weight

Weight is the "stuff" of legitimate anointing.

It is sometimes difficult to describe the boundary or edge of where the mind ends and the sudden impartation of Godly in-SIGHT begins.

There may be no internal dialogue and yet you are consciously aware that you carry the weight of the Lord. There's an aware connection with the immediate surroundings – and seemingly out of nowhere, in-SIGHT that did not come from your consciousness becomes apparent.

Spiritual sensitivity is the ability to apprehend in-SIGHT without having previous information, involvement, or attachment.

Godly in-SIGHT is the conscious alertness of new input that did not come from you.

THREE PARTS:

The variation of how you perceive and interpret is quite interesting. Nobody sees the world in the same way.

You perceive God through your giftings.

Each part of your three-fold nature (body, soul, and spirit) has the capability to receive impartation and new information. The accuracy of interpretation depends upon your WHOLENESS. We're talking about the possibility of experiencing God on all levels.

You are capable of comprehending revelation because of your senses (both redeemed natural and spiritual senses) that are operative and have been trained (Heb. 5:14).

Each person detects God's communication differently.

Some believers are more visual (receive best in seeing ways), some are auditory, and some are sensual or feeling. Each person must learn the ways that they perceive the best.

Most people tend to have one avenue of in-SIGHT that operates more dominantly than other ways. A feeling person may "sense" energies and meaning. A seeing person may generally see pictures, etc. You need to determine and then be attentive to the main ways that God speaks to you.

Spiritual in-SIGHT is, above everything else, a personal experience that cannot be created or counterfeited. Legitimate spiritual in-SIGHT can also come though (via) what your redeemed senses see, hear, or feel.

- Listen with your spiritual ears – you have ears to hear. Faith comes by hearing the *current* word (Rom. 10:17).

- LIsten with your spiritual eyes – 80% of all input is nonverbal.

- Listen with your heart - and let your senses discern.

In-SIGHT is the awareness of Christ's Presence abiding in you.

Notice that spiritual in-SIGHT reaches PAST your mind. And also notice that you must go inward to find it – to the place where distance and space lose their real meaning. After that, this apprehension is processed by your mind.

Prophetic people walk "IN" and not just "WITH" the Holy Spirit. The source of God's voice moves from exterior to interior... from being removed into being right there inside you – and fully activated and living.

As insight comes to you, make a journal and begin to practice. At first it may be glimpses or just a word. Prophecy is like a seed waiting to grow. Or like a baby waiting to be born. You must feed that Gift and bring forth that birth.

Response

Nothing can force people to listen to or cooperate with our prophetic message. Your responsibility ends with delivering the message. No one needs to obey it or even consider or interpret it.

People do not have to obey what you say. Don't feel rejected if others won't listen. You job is only to deliver it.

Guard against becoming critical when others don't understand.

If you become too "black and white" in your attitude or bring harsh delivery or judgment, it can cause a great stumbling block and sabotage the very words you have spoken.

General ministry should ultimately build and positively encourage and edify everyone. It should CONFIRM what has already been given and perhaps give additional information.

Confirmation

Prophecy should confirm what has already been given to you. BUT... this may be the first mention – and confirmation could come later. Agabus (Acts 11:27-30) prophesied a famine. The listeners prepared for it and were helped because of their obedience. They did not stock up and hoard, but rather they immediately took up a collect according to their ability.

Confirmation can come as an inner witness or knowing.

- Check to verify that it is consistent with previous Words given to you.
- If you have a negative check in your spirit or seem agitated, it could be a confirmation to NOT receive a word.

2 Peter 1:19-21, *And so we have the prophetic word confirmed, which you do well to heed as a light that shines in a dark place, until the day dawns and the morning star rises in your hearts; knowing this first, that no prophecy of Scripture is of any private interpretation, for prophecy never came by the will of man, but holy men of God spoke as they were moved (phero, carried, driven, rushed upon, upheld) by the Holy Spirit.*

Conviction

The Spirit of Truth ministers conviction (never condemnation) in order to change believers into the image and likeness Of God.

Prophecy gives us a mental image in our mind's eye and lets us see (comprehend) the unseen. Prophesy allows us to adjust and get ready. Our responsibility is to respond to that conviction with change.

You can't change another person. Only the Holy Spirit can lead them – and they decide.

"No one can persuade another to change. Each of us guards a gate of change that can only be opened from the inside. We cannot open the gate of another, either by argument or by emotional appeal." – Thomas Merton

CONDITIONAL:

If a prophecy is from the Lord, the fulfillment of THAT prophecy most often depends upon what the hearer does with it.

- There are some prophetic words that explain what the Lord is going to do regardless of human interference.

- MOST prophecy is NOT self-fulfilling. You, as the hearer, must commit to make the required choices and apply the necessary steps needed.

- Disobedience or delay can nullify that Word. If you do not meet the conditions, then God can not bless disorder.

 Each Word must be considered CONDITIONAL, even if conditions are not implied.

That means it depends on the response of human nature. This kind of prophecy is conditional upon obedience. The truth can't set people free if they don't do what is instructed!

There are other kinds of prophecy that are not dependent upon human nature but rather the plan of God that will occur regardless of what people do.

Progressive

 Events unfold and grow. Ocean currents change the landscapes over time. Winds change direction. Life emerges in the spiral of time. Things take time.

ALL public ministry should be given and received knowing that it is progressive, incomplete, and ever expanding. No single word will be the total of all that God wants to say.

Timing to Give a Word

Remember that your timing to give a word is crucial and essential! Be discerning. It is important to deliver what you have at the right time. It is okay to wait until the suitable time.

Often God desires to bring a specific word for a moment to the Body (1 Cor. 14:3, 29, Deut. 18:2).

IT MATTERS WHEN and HOW you deliver something. When someone is hurting... it is time to pour in the oil and wine.

Be assured that the prophecy is subject to the prophet. You have control over WHEN this word is released. Sometimes it is of great value to be silent. You must learn to wait for THE appropriate moment.

Should a particular time of delivery seem inappropriate, the minister in charge has the authority to ask you to hold until another (or better) time.

Ministry should flow together with a similar topic, mood, or idea. If what you have does not agree with ongoing ministry, please do not give it at that time. Quite possibly, if you wait, a better time will emerge later.

- Timing is everything. A word that comes at the wrong time is a clanging symbol. Allow the person in charge to decide if a particular time of delivery seems appropriate.

- When in doubt, write it out and turn it in to the person in charge — before or after the service.

Speaking of timing, DON'T give dates and times. Just don't. Unless you are a preeminent prophet, dates are not wise.

Fulfilment of the prophetic can occur at different time depending upon responses and choices.

Timing In Fulfillment Of A Word To You.

FULFILMENT: There is always a *process* in the fulfillment of a legitimate word. It could be instant. But, don't necessarily expect it to happen that very day. Both Abraham and David were given words that were not fulfilled in their lifetime.

There is a fullness of time required for things to happen. Often, there are times when the hearer needs to prepare himself to cause it to happen.

There may be conditions that require the cooperation of others.

What It Is NOT

As you know by now, every believer can prophesy, but not everyone holds the "Office of the Prophet." Please hear me! Just because you prophesy WELL, please do not assume that you are a 5-fold Prophet.

Excelling in a Gift, does not necessarily mean that you should start your own ministry – or even minister to everyone around. Gifts need to be seasoned and trained in the tests of fire and time.

Allow those who are mature to correct, restore, and admonish. Your job is to love and to learn.

Mature 5-fold Gift Office Prophets give a predictive word for direction, correction, confirmation, and instruction in righteousness (1 Cor. 14:29, 2 Tim. 3:16-17).

Here Are Some Imperative Guidelines:

"And I will be with your mouth, and teach you what you should say" (Ex. 4:10-11).

DURING SERVICES, it is crucial to be in agreement with the set leader. Pay attention to what is being presented by the leader.

Service time is NOT the time for you to lay hands on anybody.

Don't pray for or prophesy to anyone during the church service when others are speaking.

Please... absolutely no private ministry during service. Maintain a focused force of agreement, respect, faith, reverence, worship, prayer, and expectation with what is being presented.

What you say should synchronize with the present vision of the house.

Avoid ALL public ministry "AHEAD" of the vision of those with governmental responsibilities.

Do NOT give specific direction for the Church without speaking to leadership first and clearing the idea. Prophecies or revelatory insights (discernment, etc.) concerning the church, its direction or vision (this should be given to the main person in charge).

Prophecies for the congregation, pertaining to particular Church instructions are *ONLY* given by Church leadership.

Do not EVER rebuke an elder through prophecy.

Remember, have permission to give a public specific directive word to specific persons (the generally accepted procedure is assigned for the pre-approved, ministry staff, and visiting prophets).

Don't prophetically counsel people without leadership approval! Always respect the leaders of the house and the congregation, they may be counseling the same people.

NEVER GIVE AN ALTAR CALL (that's for the person in charge to handle).

GENERAL PROPHECY IS NOT PREDICTIVE. General prophecy is not used for foretelling the future, but to magnify God to His people.

Avoid individual correction, timing, or warning.

Be careful, my friend. Don't grandstand. You may act like what is said is a "deep truth," but reality is that unscriptural behavior turns legitimate ministries away from you.

Anytime you speak spiritual impressions to another person, make sure that it is encouraging and comforting. And, get instruction and permission before launching out.

Don't scare people about an up-coming earthquakes all over the world or cosmic disasters. Truth does not center on hell and brimstone or dark, depressing ideas of fear or grievances (social or governmental).

Don't get involved in the personal relationships of others. Don't *ever* play cupid. Don't prophetically tell someone (or even suggest) who to marry.

Certain Biblical people were married as a direct result of prophetic words. For example, Hosea and Isaac (Hosea 1:1-2, Gen. 24:40, Matt. 1:20). *Those words came from angels on assignment.* *Not you!*

Don't predict barren women to have children. There are several instances where children were predicted to be born of barren women. Samson (by angel) and John the Baptist (angel). The birth of Jesus was prophesied by angels. With the exception of Isaiah's prophecy concerning Jesus, there are no New Testament instances of babies and marriages predicted by prophets. If our Bible role models don't do that, then neither should we.

You should never predict a critical lifestyle change (like moving or leaving a job).

MONEY: Don't predict a financial decision or investments! DON'T.

NEVER manipulate with promises of money and more money – on and on. It is totally unethical and inappropriate for you to say that their money will express their faith to God so that your predicted calamity will not befall them or their families. This is absolutely unacceptable procedure.

How much money people give to you is not for you to make public. Don't cavalierly expose private information about any one

The local church is not a place for you to solicit workers, create a multi-level down line, or ask for financial support for your personal ministry.

Don't take an offering unless you are asked. The leaders probably have a plan.

Do not reveal intimate personal knowledge about someone. Jesus spoke to the Samaritan woman at the well, and His insight into her potential went beyond her obvious lifestyle. Yet, He did not condemn her, but rather released her to evangelize a city (Jn. 4).

Don't give certain or specific dates or times.

CORRECTION. You are not a CRITIC assigned to find fault or EXPOSE SIN!

Again, don't correct. You have not been given a ministry of correction (you are all backsliders... thou, thee, thy and thine are going to be straightened out in public). Leave the directive and corrective words to those in charge.

Don't give public deliverance!

RIGHT WORDS: Remember that "*The Holy Spirit speaks expressly*" (1 Tim. 4:1). To speak *expressly* means you don't ramble but speak in a plain and definitive manner.

When time is provided for prophetic interaction, remember, you are only responsible to give and to share what God speaks to you... and no more. Once you release that, don't add anything else!

Speak words that are easy to understand (not a lot of Christianese). Do not speak in King James English – God communicates in your language!

"Think like a wise man but communicate in the language of the people."
William Butler Yeats

 Be sure you communicate what God is telling you NOW. Not last week, not yesterday. Not what you heard someone else prophesy or say on TV.

Caution when using the Gifts there is responsibility that goes with it.

NEVER HAUGHTY OR SELF EXALTING. Get yourself out of the message. Completely. Your method of delivery should never be overbearing or proud. Be careful not to think too highly of yourself – or take the credit. Everyone should serve the church's greater call as a prophetic community.

God gives some people the ability to see and hear things that others do not. Sometimes this type of person is not gifted with great oral ability to express themselves, but they should give that information – even if it is only a single word or phrase.

Allow yourself to have in-SIGHT, even if it's only a single word or phrase. Speak clearly and naturally. Be simple. Extravagant deliveries self-promote.

We find much damage from "PROPHETIC FISHING" techniques. One guy I knew said things like, "I see November – what does that mean?" Do you have a child born that month? If the answer is *YES*, he says, "Well that child will be put in prison." OR *NO, he says,* "Your child will be sick in that month." *Psychic readers do this all the time.*

Never disclose extremely personal information in your prophetic ministry.

Above All – Speak LIFE

"The tongue has the power of life and death" (Prov. 18:21). "Today I have given you the choice between life and death, between blessings and curses. Now I call on heaven and earth to witness the choice you make. Oh, that you would choose life, so that you and your descendants might live! (Deut. 30:19).

If you are prophesying, please don't repeat the doom and gloom predictions like many of the more "famous prophets" - instead, speak LIFE. Your words should always bring spirit and life! Change the way things are.

This topic is being repeated because MANY of our Prophetic Leaders are agreeing with the adversary.

Apostolic influence agrees with the will of God! LIFE. Safety. Peace. We have been given creation power with our words! Choose this day – life or death. Believe your words have power to change.

 Speak out of the THIRD heaven! Amen. Come up higher. Don't prophesy out of the Second heaven... don't minister to the fallen Adam. Bring heaven to earth!

This is a VERY SERIOUS problem in the church. People are unknowingly granting power and speaking forth negative possibilities rather than moving from an apostolic position of influence.

Call what is not as though it is! (Rom. 4:17) God's intention must be declared.

Your insight should never be distracted by what you see on the outside.

'He [the Messiah] will not judge by what he sees with his eyes, or decide by what he hears with his ears' (Isaiah 11:3). That means you don't fore-tell the gloom and doom future.

- If you see that someone is heading for trouble, speak the way of clarity for their safety.

- You must not minister out of your own "feelings" toward a person or a situation – but rather seek for the plan and purpose of the Lord. Allow His concepts to intimately change your impressions.

The response to the idea of speaking LIFE is often met with great opposition. I encouraged one guy recently who was prophesying misery and kid-napping over someone. He was infuriated with the idea, "I have walked in the prophetic for over 20 years," he yelled. "I speak what I am told to speak, whether positive and uplifting according to man's feelings...or not. If it is a harsh corrective word, a chiding one, or a pep rally speech. Should I filter the message? "

The answer is YES! Remember, it is through your own personal filter that you hear and interpret the Spirit of God. WHY do you know this informa-tion? To agree with it or to change the situation by your words of power and influence?

Agree with what the Spirit says. Don't go past the "green light." Know for sure that the Spirit of God speaks LIFE.

If you see harm, speak life. Don't tell me I'm going to die in a car wreck this afternoon, declare safety over my travels. If you see conflict, speak resolution. If you see back biting and jealously, speak reconciliation to that matter.

If I know that some man is badly gossiping about his pastor, a good word to him is that he is now chained to the pastor's leg and brought into this house as an example to serve and bless the pastor in deep covenant! And that as this covenant grows, advancement and success will surely come. Of course, the gossiper probably knows that you know – but he is spared embarrassment and is given a genuine challenge from the Lord.

Call what is not as though it is.

The important thing to remember here is that if you sense disaster in someone's life, take authority over it and turn the tide. Don't let a person think they are going to die when you can speak creative words to protect them.

 Don't speak out of a second heaven or soul realm perspective – where what you know or think is confused with God's intention. The Finished Work shows you that evil has been overcome by the Cross. Speak Victory and Overcoming.

The impartation comes into your spirit man. But, it is processed by our souls and delivered by our body (mouth). That's why it is important to transform and renew ourselves. A received word must be processed correctly.

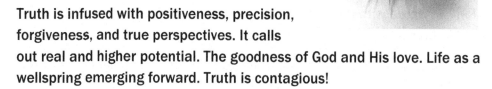

Truth is infused with positiveness, precision, forgiveness, and true perspectives. It calls out real and higher potential. The goodness of God and His love. Life as a wellspring emerging forward. Truth is contagious!

CAUTIONS ABOUT <u>RECEIVING</u> PROPHETIC MINISTRY

It is totally awesome to receive a genuine word from God that will define your purpose and answer questions.

Jesus told us that anyone who receives a prophet will receive a prophet's reward (Matt. 10:41a). That means that God wants us to receive prophecy in order to receive rewards. We must give room for the learning and development of this gift. We must allow opportunity for believers to become accomplished with their gift.

We cannot stereotype the way you should receive from God... everyone is different in their function. However, there are some guidelines of ministry that must be within the boundaries of apostolic/prophetic order –meaning "not out of order." With all that in mind there are some precautions:

Love it. Despise it not.

Don't receive a prophetic word from just everybody without trying it.

Do not allow others to prophetically share their need for you to support their ministry or their financial needs. Don't pay to receive a prophecy.

Keep a personal prophetic journal. Always look for patterns and themes that incorporate several words. You will find the total message precept by precept, here a little and there a little (Is. 28:10).

BE PATIENT: DON'T EXPECT THE ANSWER TODAY!

Ps. 118-9 says that Until the time that his word came to pass, the word of the Lord tested him. NIV says, "Till the word of the Lord proved him true." Joseph waited for 13 years in a foreign land for the promise to come to pass.

- Word = commandment, speech, or word.

- Tested = to be refined as by a metal smith.
- The Word of God tested Joseph the same way that metal smiths remove impurities, and forge swords in a refinery.

Joseph was sold into slavery, falsely accused by Potiphar's wife. He was put in prison again. He ministered to those in prison during that time... But, the cup bearer didn't mention him for awhile. He was busy and forgot. The dream and vision in Joseph's heart was tried.

Just because you are ready doesn't mean that others are.

It is a process to go through as the Word is fulfilled. Walking into the promise means a renewing and regenerating of the mind. It is a graduation, promotion... perfect positioning - on God's timetable.

God will not tempt us, but we are tried. Perseverance works patience. A true word is a covenant... it is an oath on God's part. It is a promise that won't be broken. Our part is the process to stand and walk it out. Wait.

You should never make a critical lifestyle change (like getting married, moving, or leaving a job) solely on the basis of prophetic ministry from another person. You must have an internal witness.

Prophecy should CONFIRM WHAT GOD HAS ALREADY TOLD YOU.

You need to learn to hear for yourself. Don't be a "prophecy junkie!" In other words, don't become prophetically dependent. Don't habitually depend or NEED prophetic ministry to make decisions. God plans to reveal Himself personally to you. Don't lean on "words" from others for your sole guidance.

Don't depend on personal ministry, or that someone will have "a word for you." In general, the Holy Spirit plans to reveal Himself personally as you pray and study.

Don't try to make a prophecy say what you want to hear. God's legitimate messages will consistently say what God says, not what you want Him to say. Don't twist words to fit your own way.

Be in accountability. Allow proper discernment and evaluation. Let the revelatory gifts bring the breath of God to quicken that Word into your heart.

Don't allow yourself to attach to certain people because you think that they can prophetically guide you. This reliance could border on spiritism – and it is VERY dangerous.

Resist the temptation to engage in relationships that foster positions of power or dependence.

FLATTERY: Don't allow yourself to be entreated by words of flattery. Remember the story of Jeroboam and the old prophet. The young man died because he listened to illegitimate prophecy and he disobeyed the previous instructions of the angel (1 Kings 13:18). This young man who was destined to become a prophet, allowed flattery to kill him.

Refuse to receive personal "closet" directives – whether they be on the telephone, or in private meetings. "Parking lot prophets" can potentially cause tremendous damage while inflating their own egos.

Such ministries will NOT be endorsed or encouraged in most places. Guard yourself from receiving words that could hinder or mislead you. Self-appointed ministers sometimes operate in error, vanity, and rebellion. They often choose to not be accountable. This could cause you much confusion and distrust.

Beware of those who use prophecy in an attempt to separate you from the accountability structure of the local church. Proverbs 18:1 warns you against those practices. Know those who minister to you.

"I appeal to you, brethren, to be on your guard concerning those who create dissensions and difficulties and cause divisions, in opposition to the doctrine (the teaching) which you have been taught. [I warn you to turn aside from them, to] avoid them. For such persons do not serve our Lord Christ but their own appetites and base desires, and by ingratiating (good words) and flattering speech, they beguile (deceive) the hearts of the unsuspecting and simpleminded [people]" (Rom. 16:17-18 AMP).

Be guarded against "smooth sayings" and those prophesying out of their own imaginations.

> *"Now the Spirit speaks expressly, that in the latter times some shall depart from the faith, giving heed to seducing spirits, and doctrines of devils"* (1 Tim. 4:1).

Be sure to remain supernaturally natural! And naturally spiritual.

Don't Use A Premeditated Offense or Previous Knowledge

> *"I solemnly charge you in the presence of God and of Christ Jesus and of His chosen angels, to maintain these principles without bias, doing nothing in a spirit of partiality or judgement"* (1 Tim. 5:21).

Matthew 18 says you GO to the person and speak to them if you have offense. Don't EVER minister to someone about an offense you have!

Generally speaking, prophetic words should be spontaneous, not premeditated. If you have previous knowledge of an event, or discussion with others about a third party - you do not go the third party to correct them without hearing their side.

You do not say that it is a WORD from God if you have previous knowledge about an incident. Just express your opinion.

If you sense that you have something to share about a situation that <u>you know about already</u>, then, you should say something like, "I heard about...... and the Lord stirred my heart. I feel I should share with you...." etc.

A GREAT caution must be forcefully declared that your "Gifts" don't give you permission to mistreat and/or embarrass people. Any arrogant tendency to discard people who don't do or say what you want... is not fitting for anyone in ministry.

HELPING KIDS TO PROPHESY:

This of course, is a whole new and exciting topic.

- Teach kids about the Bible
- Teach kids to speak what they believe God is saying to them.
- Pray for kids that their prophetic gifts will be activated. Prophesy to them.
- Ask your kids about their dreams and have them tell what they mean.
- Teach them Guidelines and Protocol.

ACCOUNTABILITY

SIGNS THAT YOU MAY NOT BE ACCOUNTABLE INCLUDE:

- Operating in your gifts and ministries in isolation

- Not being open to correction or adjustment, or

- Believing you are directly accountable to God only is an Old Testament perspective.

Why You Want Prophetic Accountability

Accountability expectations may vary from leader to leader, but it provides a way to maintain Guidelines and Protocol. It maintains the boundaries of this assembly – meaning not "out of order" at that particular place.

Accountability in the prophetic should be to someone who is more proficient in this Gift and who will honor the Gift and also give you valuable input.

Accountability acts as a safety net to protect you from yourself and from making mistakes. Everyone has "blind spots' that others can see and help them with. Growth and improvement come as we find proper accountably and mentoring – while retaining a teachable attitude.

NEW TESTAMENT PRECEDENT. Paul gave instruction concerning prophetic accountability and guidelines (1 Cor 14, 1 Thess. 5, Acts 14:26-28, 18:22).

Paul received a direct revelation concerning his ministry to the Gentiles. Yet, he submitted the revelation to James and the leaders in Jerusalem (Gal. 1:1-2).

We have talked a lot about how prophetic ministry is not just about the fact that you receive revelation – it's about how you interpret it, how you communicate it, when you say it, and to whom. Though we are not the same, there are standards.

Accountability helps you properly process your insights. (1 Cor 14:29, 1 Thess 5:20-21).

Accountability Empowers the Church to act as a God Intends

Accountability enhances your delivery and you interpretation.

Accountability keeps your pride in check.

> 'Where there is strife, there is pride, but wisdom is found in those who take advice' (PROV 13:10, 1 Pet. 5:5b).

Accountability helps us all work together as one body and combine our efforts toward major goals. It also combines Gifts to bring even greater manifestations.

Don't be a maverick! Be ready to grow. Make yourself accountable. Many more doors of opportunity and acceptance will come to you when you are KNOWN and are in covenant with those who are set as leaders.

Develop relationships with the local church leaders and they will gladly recognize, encourage, and promote your gifts. It is always best to get consent from them and be released and acknowledged as needed.

Everyone needs accountability to another person in leadership or to a team (Acts 20:28). All revelatory-gifted people should link themselves within relationships of accountability, protection, and mentoring. It's important to be in mutual submission and *koininea* relationship with/to others. Yield to one another's gifts. *Be connected AND IN COVENANT with Apostolic/prophetic leadership.*

> Your gifts can be enhanced by someone who already does it. Remember that Anna (who was a prophet) glorified God, while Simeon (who was not called a prophet) prophesied (Lk. 2:29-32).

To be effective, genuine prophetic accountability must include:

ANSWERABILITY: (Gal 2:1-2). You can report to someone concerning revelation (insights) that you receive from God.

TRANSPARENCY: (Eph 4:25) You are open and not secretive about that which may be relevant to the process.

TEACHABILITY: (Acts 18:26) You are willing to learn and improve.

DEFERRING: (Heb 13:17) There are times when you obey Biblical leaders and their directives even when you don't totally understand.

Mistakes

If you do try to minister with the gifts, you will make a mistake. We all have made mistakes.

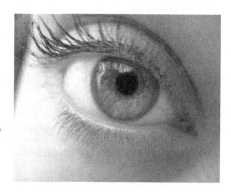

The old story goes that one pastor said, "God said, just as Noah led the children out of Egypt"...silence.... "Thus saith the Lord, I didn't say that – ahhh... Just as Moses...."

Some self-appointed prophets make ridiculous mistakes that continuously violate prophetic principles. As we love and instruct them, we must also raise the banner of prophetic expectations even higher. By maintaining correct order, we raise mature, seasoned, and accurate prophets who operate with a measure of wisdom.

Many years ago, I was speaking at a church and a Bishop came up to me at the end of the service and told me publicly that God said, "Get your house in order, for tomorrow you will die."

I had to spend the next hour correcting that pronouncement of death, because I had NO intention of dying - yet. And obviously (and thankfully), I'm still here!

A GREAT problem in the church today is that very well known "prophets" have clearly said things that never happened. They never adjusted or corrected that mistake and now they have lost respect and validation.

You MUST simply ADMIT it and take responsibility for your own miscommunications – even accidental ones. If you make a mistake – just ADMIT IT and go forward (1 Peter 5:5).

Anybody can make unintentional mistakes and be wrong. Scripture explains that we "see through a glass darkly" (1 Cor. 13:12). Accuracy develops with practice.

Instruction and learning to excel does not diminish us, anymore than waiting could diminish a pregnant mother. We are enlarged in the waiting and strengthened through instruction. Of course, we don't always see the Tree of LIFE that is developing within us. But the more we are instructed, the more enlarged is our expectancy.

Proper ministry will be encouraged and acknowledged, while improper uses should be adjusted. It is best to give the first correction in private, if possible. (However, if this word could bring confusion to a group, then you may have to kindly correct it right away).

When someone cares about you, then instruction is embraced. We value the opportunity to give you instruction that will cause you to excel in your ministry. All instruction should be viewed as helpful and as an opportunity to grow.

Proper instruction will bring maturing to know what, how, when, and why to prophesy and how to relate your Gift to the Body.

Judging a word!

Be assured that correction doesn't come from just anyone that happens to be around – the only ones to "judge" will be the "set leader" of the meeting or those with a recognized prophetic ministry.

 "Let the OTHERS (literally, that means "other prophets of the SAME KIND" - not everybody) judge" (1 Cor. 14:29). Don't miss this. Everyone is not to judge – only those who are also prophets.

Please be open TO LEARN to flow with the body in this manner. Allow yourself to have mentors – learn to excel.

Judging sometimes requires an assembling of related factors into the whole!

Together, let's learn to excel!

If a message won't stand up to scrutiny, don't give it. Be ready to learn to excel!

Be teachable! Learn from past mistakes. Keep going. Excitedly embrace correction as a protection and also a way to perfect your gifts.

Excelling in the Prophetic!

"Prophecy is the immediate message of God to His people through a divinely anointed utterance." J. Lopez

Prophecy is the voice of God released to create, built, renew, re-form, re-organize, re-structure, and realign. But remember, you are not just ONE singular Gift. Everyone flows in several... We cannot discuss the details of the individual gifts in great depth, but merely provide an overview.

1 Corinthians 13:9 says that you *"prophesy in part"* and all see through a glass darkly. If you have a PART, then that part may well fit together with other parts.

It is a mixture of revelation and your interpretation. We begin to birth the Word of God, and it develops as we proceed. The Amplified translation states, "For our knowledge is fragmentary (incomplete and perfect), and your prophecy... is fragmental (incomplete and imperfect).Paul tells us to *prophesy in proportion to the faith given to us.* That means the Lord will pull up from your spirit the parts of revelational deposit that He needs at a given moment in order to speak to the present moment – and that others may also have a piece of that same truth!

Character

The prophetic gift bypasses the mind and flows from the Spirit. That does not mean it is mindless. People who flow well in prophecy have also renewed their mind so that they can deliver the word of God with accuracy.

John 14:26 says that the Comforter brings all things to remembrance. That is the Greek word *hupomimnesko* meaning that the revealed words were known and now recalled.

Hearing from God should be a daily and natural occurrence. We should learn to bring edification, exhortation, and comfort in everything that we speak.

You can't transform cities and nations until you are transformed within yourself as individuals

God's change agents are His believers.

You can not EARN Gifts. But you can improve your character.

The natural person whose mind is set on things of this world cannot receive the things of the Spirit (1 Cor. 2:14, Rom. 8:5-6). Do you believe that? If so, there are adjustments that need to be made! Right?

The objective here is to determine how character and WHOLENESS augment the prophetic delivery and interpretation of revelation. We have established that when we are born again, we received (already) all of Christ, His character, His mind, His existence, His anointing, and even His gifts which are offices and ministries awaiting maturity.

As our soul and mind are redeemed, we *"are complete (WHOLE, undivided, complete, inner-connected, and unified) in Him"* (Col. 2:10).

We can be whole and a baby. A baby coconut is whole and has everything inside that it needs to become a tree. It needs to grow.

〓〓

It is imperative to learn how to INTER-PRET and DELIVER spiritual matters in a more complete way. Character development is the answer. Revelatory people need to sharpen their skills and develop more integrity and accuracy. Credibility and preciseness are essential.

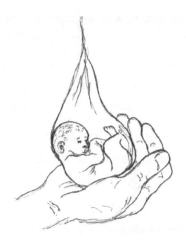

Continued training and practice causes you to increase your discernment skills. It's necessary to try to capture these moments on a daily basis. By raising the level of your skill and maturity, you can comprehend in-SIGHTS that may come in several forms and with many interpretations and applications.

In my book, "Apostolic Authority" it talks about how POWER (*dunamis*) is the force of God, but AUTHORITY (*exousia*) is the "right to use that power." Right character increases your authority to speak for God.

These resident (inherited) gifts have nothing to do with your spiritual condition or character. That's why you sometimes see people who have great gifts, but live outrageously.

What you must accomplish is a mature character that will handle your gifts with credibility and trustworthiness.

Character provides the safety that we need. It's by the FRUIT OF THE SPIRIT that your true gifts are perfected and matured.

YOUR GIFTS[1]

Gifts enable others to experience God's HEART in the present. What is God's plan? How will He pour out His life through them? Being part of a Gift of the Spirit puts you in a "flash point" between two kingdoms. You enter into the overlapping CO-EXISTING space where accurate Gifts operate.

Gifts of the Spirit cause you to perceive and experience the NOW INTENTION and purpose of God in your life.

Optimum use of the Gifts of the Spirit emphasizes what God would release and receive through His mature sons. The Gifts should not center on what people need, but should creatively reveal God's ultimate INTENTION.

Gifts enable others to experience God's heart in the present. We must be consistent, deliberate, definite, and conscientious in expressing the words that express the heart of the Lord.

Briefly speaking, GIFTS are sovereignly given by God severally as He wills (1 Cor. 12:11) and they are resident in us from the beginning, as God desires.

> We don't earn them or choose them, but the USE and release of them is a consequence of freely receiving our inheritance in Christ.

> Gifts are not preoccupied with isolated parts of truth but are and positioned so that we can properly relate the WHOLE with all the parts.

> *Possession of a Gift isn't a measure of the quality of your faith.*

Go out into the world uncorrupted, a breath of fresh air in this squalid and polluted society. Provide people with a glimpse of good living and of the

---

1. This section is partly from my book, "Connecting." http://www.kluane.com/index.php/products/books

living God. Carry the LIGHT-GIVING MESSAGE into the night
(Phil. 2:15 MSG).

Your Gifts can be enhanced, activated, trained, and deepened toward their fullest potential through the pursuit of truth, honesty, integrity, and developed through proper mentoring (1 Ki. 19:15- 21, 2 Ki. 2:1-15, Lk. 10: 1-11, 19, Heb. 5:14). Possession of a Gift is not an index or measure of the quality of our faith – it is a challenge to faithful use.

Other Scriptures relating to Prophecy: 1 Sam. 3:19-21, 2 Chron 20:20, Amos 3:7, Matt. 10:41, 1 Cor. 12:28, 13:8-10, 1 Cor. Chapter 14, Eph. 2:19-20, E4:11, 1 Pet. 4:11, 2 Pet. 1:19-21

Gifts of the Holy Spirit:

- Given by the Spirit (1 Cor. 12 &14).
- Given to all (1 Cor. 14:24, 31) in various levels according to Divine purpose.
- Given to the body for the common good (1 Cor. 12:7)
- Given to the members (1 Cor. 12:12, 14-26).
- Speaks of past and present (1 Cor. 12:8-10).
- Delivers the Word (1 Cor. 14:12)
- Speaks to the church (1 Cor. 14:2-4)
- Speaks of Grace

Each of the Gifts following can be used to prophesy.

You need to interpret or translate what God gives you in a way that communicates to others.

The Gifts of the Holy Spirit (as in 1 Cor. 12 above) are essential to living successfully. Gifts of the Spirit are DIVIDED INTO THREE DISTINCT PARTS by the different words for "*another*" in the Greek. (This is NOT generally the way these groups are presented.)

However, Paul divided them in this manner: 1) The first part, the word of wisdom and word of knowledge. 2) To *ANOTHER* (of different part) the gift of faith, healings, to *ANOTHER* (of same part as group 2) gifts of working of miracles, prophecy, and (same part group 2) discerning of spirits. 3) To *ANOTHER* (of a different part) tongues and interpretation of tongues (1 Cor. 12). See below:

1st Part – GIFTS Redeemed INTELLECT Revelation	2nd Part– to ANOTHER GIFTS OF FAITH	3rd Part – to Another GIFTS RELATED
Word of Wisdom	Healings, & Gift of faith Working of Mira-cles	Tongues
Word of Knowledge	Prophecy	Interpretation of Tongues
	Discerning of Spirits	

These Gifts illuminate and reveal His capacity, power, and what He wants us to know. Each Gift can be used prophetically. Each genuine use of the Gift makes heaven perceptible NOW.

Gifts come to bless others.

Received gifts can be developed (Heb. 5:14).

The Gifts of the Spirit are nine different methods that God uses to communicate (via His LANGUAGE and mode of expression).

GIFTS FROM	GIFTS given and not earned:
GOD THE FATHER gives Gift OPERATIONS	Rom. 12:6: God gives gifts differing (for ministry). Prophet, minister, teacher, exhorter, encourager, giver, leader, government, mercy shower. These OPERATIONS and activities demonstrate dimensional Kingdom principles which enable and complete the FATHER'S INTENTION.
GOD THE SON gives GIFT OFFICES	Eph. 4:11: Jesus gives the grace GIFT OFFICE ministries which are the apostles, prophets, evangelists, and pastor/ teachers. God's government brings forth His vision, mission, and purpose of GOD'S SON to the generations.
GOD THE HOLY SPIRIT gives GIFTS	1 Cor. 12: THE HOLY SPIRIT gives ABILITIES: a Word of wisdom, word of knowledge, faith, healings, working of miracles, prophecy, discerning of spirits, tongues, interpretations of tongues. The Holy Spirit decides the measure and manner by which we express this spiritual language that relates heavenly ideals, patterns, and imperatives.

Prophetic Music and the Song of The Lord

I call to remembrance my song in the night; I meditate within my heart, and my spirit makes diligent search (Ps. 77:6).

1 Chronicles 25 describes a seer operating in temple music, *"Moreover David and the captains of the host separated to the service of the sons of Asaph, and of Heman, and of Jeduthun, who should prophesy with harps, with psalteries, and with cymbals: and the number of the workmen according to their service was."*

Musicians can deliver visions, dreams, and insights in song. Often times, music is a most extraordinary way to connect to the Lord and to the congregation in intercession and praise. It can be a vehicle to receive and deliver revelation.

In prophetic music, it is also important to have ORDER and accountability. *Of the sons of Asaph; Zaccur, and Joseph, and Nethaniah, and Asarelah, the sons of Asaph under the hands of Asaph, which PROPHESIED*

ACCORDING TO THE ORDER OF THE KING. Of Jeduthun: the sons of Jeduthun; Gedaliah, and Zeri, and Jeshaiah, Hashabiah, and Mattithiah, six, UNDER THE HANDS OF THEIR FATHER Jeduthun, who prophesied with a harp, to give thanks and to praise the LORD" (1 Chron. 25:2-3).

Singing is the mouthpiece of the SOUL. And, this is one of the best ways to start out in public ministry!

All through time, people of faith "sang a new song," especially when they understood or perceived another aspect of God's character (Heb. 2:12, Rev. 19:10).

A New Song is unrehearsed and spontaneous.

Every day, as you increase your understanding of God's truth and upgrade your reality into new levels of Glory, you can "sing a new song."

> After Miriam crossed the Red Sea and sang, the swarming mass of Israelites stepped upon dry ground and began to arrange themselves into organized tribes with defined function.

> David sang many of his petitions and praises.

The Bible is full of songs! Singers led the wars. There were songs of songs, triumph, marching, working, building, watchmen, love songs, wedding songs, drinking songs, dance songs, palace songs, harlot songs, sorrow songs, songs of the night, songs of deliverance,

The desert sings, waste places sing, mountains and hills, the rocks, the sea, the stars, the islands, birds, trees, all sing.

It's not just about new rhythmic and catchy lyrics. It's a song that communicates about the ever-revealing God Who shows more of Himself everyday.

New Songs can reiterate the message of the day!

As continuing truths are grasped, your songs release understanding to others around the world. You begin to look like the One you sing about. His character is reproduced in you. Your passion ignites others to sing with you.

Prophetic songs can describe what happens when you obtain deliverance from old ways. They can describe your unshackling, declare "who" you perceive yourself to be, and tell "how" you overcome all obstacles.

Whenever a release of new understanding or a new insight happens, it is appropriate to have the accompanying sound of this message enforced by melodious harmonies that reiterate the revelatory intents of God.

- "New songs" discharge the true purposes of God's plans.
- Songs proclaim the victory of the Finished Work.
- "New songs" unleash prophetic direction and guidance. New songs bring emancipation from dead (religious) places and usher rivers of quickened newness.

Don't analyze each word, but let the river begin. Expect new lyrics that have never been sung and new melodies never heard before. Discover new tempos and sounds waiting to be revealed through us.

What Kind of Songs to Sing?

You may sing spiritual songs that are prophetic messages.

Songs should be at the same frequency as the declaration. Never ritual, but new declarations. Songs should be consistent with melody given. Songs should be sung by those who can sing in tune.

- Try to sing in an unrehearsed nature.

- Sing Scriptures.

- Create resident anthems for your church!

- Sing and respond to what God has done.

- Recount God's gracious ways and acts.

- Give thanks and praise to Him.

To Whom?

Songs can be from a believer to communicate a message to the Church.

Songs can be from a believer to God.

Songs can be FROM GOD speaking to the congregation.

Songs should move progressively from being ABOUT Jesus to being TO HIM as the fellowship deepens.

Purposes of the Song of the Lord

- Helps to bring the total man into total worship

- Brings people closer into God's presence

- Brings the Church up to Mount Zion

- Releases a prophetic mantle

- Releases the Gifts of the Spirit

- Cleanses and prepares the congregation to hear the Word

- Causes believers to be more God conscious

- Gets the Word of God in your mind

- Reveals the character of God

- Remembers the promises of God

- Offers spiritual sacrifices

- Gives God glory

"Sing to him a NEW SONG; play skillfully, and shout for joy" (Ps 33:3 NIV).

"He put a NEW SONG in my mouth, A hymn of praise to our God. Many will see and fear and put their trust in the LORD" (Ps 40:3 NIV).

"Sing to the LORD a NEW SONG; sing to the LORD, all the earth. Sing to the LORD, praise His name; proclaim his salvation day after day. Declare His glory among the nations, His marvelous deeds among all peoples" (Ps. 96:1 NIV).

Also see: Isa. 42:10-13, Ps. 98:1; Ps. 126:1-3; Ps 144:9; Ps 149:1, 1 Chron. 13:6-8

Rev. 5:9-10, "And they sang a NEW SONG: 'You are worthy to take the scroll and to open its seals... you have made them to be a kingdom and priests to serve our God.'"

Rev 5:9, "And they sang a NEW SONG: "You are worthy to take the scroll and to open its seal thereof... "(see also Rev. 14:1-3, 15-16).

This topic can also easily be a book.

How You Can Be "LED"

We've been talking about how the Lord God communicates any way He wants. Each of you must discover your personal encoded Gifting that will communicate to others and release them into identity and purpose.

NOTE: The purpose of this book is not to create an in-depth search on this subject of particular Gifts, only to provide the following reference guide.[2]

The Lord always speaks to you as a friend (Jn. 15:15).

You can be LED through IMPRESSIONS: It's important to know that 95% of your spiritual communication is NOT AUDIBLE and NOT VISIBLE. Most of the time, you connect with God through an inner impression or senses by the INNER WITNESS of His Spirit. This type of in-SIGHT usually comes as spontaneous thought, feeling, or impression.

---

2. **See my book, "Connecting."** http://www.kluane.com/index.php/products/books

Have you ever been doing one thing and then had an impression to start doing something else? Paul was just walking along, when he "saw" a man who had faith to be healed (Acts 14:9).

- When Einstein discovered the theory of relativity, he said that it was revealed to him after an intense period of research and logical reasoning as in an "intuitive flash."

Sometimes impressions are called INTUITION: This is the ability of attaining quick and ready information without rational thought or factual study. This immediate knowing may also be a gut feeling, a dramatic warning, or caution.

It may be like "a divine hunch" concerning a future event or result. For example, my grandfather suddenly had a strong urge to not get on the regular train to go home after work. That train crashed. If he had gotten on that train, my mother would not have been born, and I would not be writing this book!

- A "gut reaction" is an intuitive response to a person or situation, which involves aroused instincts. It is an immediate response without forethought.

Intuition can also be called a Godly PREMONITION. This is the compelling urge, knowing, inner warning, or expected anticipation of an event without conscious reasoning or facts to back it up.

You can be LED through DISCERNING of Spirits. This is not the gift of criticism nor the Gift of Discernment. Discerning of Spirits recognizes both good and evil, right and wrong. On the other hand, the purpose of the Gift of Discerning of Spirits is not just to find the devil in someone or something, but rather to identify the deposit of Christ!

Discerning of Spirits is a supernatural revelation of the activities of the Spirit realm.

Discernment is INSIGHT (1 Cor. 12:10) that can come from three forms.

Discernment of the human heart.

Discernment of spiritual activity.

Discernment of what the Holy Spirit is saying and doing.

You can be LED through an INNER WITNESS or KNOWINGS. Sometimes there can be a deep "knowing" in your spirit about something. This can be a "feeling" or in-SIGHT independent of your knowledge or facts available. "The Spirit will show you things to come" (Jn. 16:13).

All believers experience this inner witness of inspiration. Romans 9:1, "I am not lying, my conscience also bearing me witness in the Holy Spirit." This is the mind of Christ expressing itself in us.

He who believes in the Son of God has a witness in himself (Jn. 4:10). An inner witness is often a doorway into other Gifts of the Spirit.

You can suddenly have an understanding about a Scripture, or a problem. You can know to take food to the neighbor, or call someone on the phone, or pray with someone about a specific need. The more you mature in these knowings, the more they will happen (Mk. 2:8-9).

All believers can experience this refreshing inner witness of *knowing*. Romans 9:1 says, *"My conscience also bearing me witness in the Holy Spirit."* This happens when the mind of Christ expresses itself in us. 1 John 5:10 explains it further, *"He who believes in the Son of God has a witness IN himself."* An inner witness can be the doorway into releasing a Word of Knowledge or Discerning of Spirits.

Many times, revelatory people just "know" or "feel" that something is going to happen. This kind of in-SIGHT is obtained spontaneously without conscious inquiry. You might call it a "gut feeling" or a "sixth sense" about something. It is a sudden awareness or phenomenon that can be experienced by all. Here again, you see how sensory feelings can link to spiritual activation (Matt. 14:14, Jn. 2:17).

A feeling: We can receive inspiration through the emotions and in our bodies (again why it is so important to consecrate ourselves). This type can be mistaken... that's why we submit ourselves to mature believers to learn.

An Impression: A feeling or sense. The still small voice. This is what Paul explained when he said that we may all prophesy... we can all express what we perceive from God. Some believers have had a dormant or hidden gift that needs to be unearthed at this time. "Oh, that all the Lord's people were prophets (nabiy) and that the Lord would put His Spirit upon them" (Numb. 11:29).

You can be LED through your SENSES. Like X-ray vision, seeing a picture, smelling, hearing a word or message.

You can be LED through the REPETITION OF EVENTS. God may decide to underline by repetition (echo effect) a message so that you cannot ignore it.

You can be LED through the SPECTACULAR. Few and far between are those unique times when you see the lightning bolts, have hot coals on your lips, see angels flying, or watch the Glory cloud settle. This may be the way you want it all the time... but the spectacular is rarely the case.

If you are involved in spectacular moments, then you must know that it is a sovereign opportunity – and it's not The Lord's way of everyday leading. Do not be anxious about having spectacular moments. People who always look for another mystical encounter often make tragic mistakes.

You can be LED through MIRACLES. Miracles can inspire you to great in-SIGHT.

You can be LED through INSPIRATION. (Heb.1:1; 2 Tim. 3:16, 17, 2 Peter 1:20,21). Spiritual in-SIGHT and inspiration can slip in unexpectedly. It happens to me a lot in the car, when I'm just driving along and singing softly. Then suddenly, something triggers – and it seems out of nowhere a connection comes with the answers I need.

True inspiration touches the depths of God and gives you a clear heart-felt experience with the living Jesus..... This kind of genuine close encounter WILL forever change the direction of your life.

You can be LED by SYNCHRONICITY. This describes what people some-times inaccurately call "coincidence." Synchronicity (or serendipity) always involves a crucial time element. It pertains to a God planned interaction between two people or parallel events that occur without your intervention or previous plan of hooking together.

Synchronicity is where God's plans and your plans and actions converge. It sometimes links you to objective events in the external world (i.e., "acci-dentally being in the right place at the right time). This is one of the most recognizable of all manifestations.

You can be "LED" through HEARING. As the first couple heard the voice of the Lord in the Garden, we, the arising Bridal company in the last hour, should fully expect the total restoration of this ability to hear with pro-found clarity. How will you hear?

You can be LED through the VOICE or confession of your human person. You can purposefully speak and confess the Word. Mary proclaimed her agreement, "Be it unto me according to Your Word" (Lk. 1:38). This isn't confessing an extravagant convertible, but rather creatively declaring God's purposes into this dimension.

You can be LED through the spontaneous VOICE of your own words. Some-times you can say words that did not seem to come from your conscious-ness. This can become a major way of hearing the Almighty.

You can be LED through the VOICE of your inner self. A very common method of in-SIGHT for most people is the ongoing inner voice and internal conversation.

You can be LED through the SCRIPTURES, SERMONS, LEADERS, OBSERV-ERS, HUMAN MESSENGERS, and CONVERSATIONS with OTHERS. Prepare to hear the Lord through others – whether they be your minister, a child, a grandparent, the person in your office that bugs you, or a prisoner in jail. In-SIGHT can come from the most unlikely places. However, you need to discern what is said.

1 Samuel 1:12-13 tells how the old priest Eli misread Hannah's intentions because he watched her mouth and didn't understand because Hannah SPOKE FROM HER HEART. Eli couldn't hear Hannah's heart because he only looked at the natural.

You need to look and listen to other's hearts. Something totally fantastic happens when you connect with another person on a deep spiritual level.

You can be LED Through IMPARTATION. The apostle Paul tells the Roman church (1:11), "For I long to see you, that I may impart (give over, share) unto you some SPIRITUAL GIFT (*pneumatikos charismakos*), to the end you may be established" (KJV). We see that Apostles have the ability to impart spiritual gifts to help establish the church.

Impartation can come also from Mentoring... even reading this book can actually become an impartation. You are studying under the person who wrote it! Finding mentors to train you is one of the best ways to learn.

You can be LED through an INAUDIBLE VOICE from the Lord. A still small voice (1 Kings 19:11-13) is quiet, but not illusive or vague. This "delicate whispering voice" (NKJ) is one of the easiest ways to clearly hear from God. It comes without prompting and you hear it with your spiritual ears.

You can be LED through an AUDIBLE VOICE to you alone. You may hear audible revelation that's not heard by others (spirit to spirit) (Gen. 3:9-10,

Deut. 4:13, Ex. 19:9, Jn. 12:28). Paul was knocked to the ground from off his horse and heard an audible voice (Acts 9:3-7). The others nearby did not see or hear anything.

- The voice of the Lord can be manifested in the natural realm of hearing. Jesus said that His sheep hear His voice (Jn. 10:27, Rev. 3:20). It is the inner-man that hears and interprets this voice.

- In Scripture, the audible voice can come from behind (Ex. 3:12, 2 Kg. 7:5-7, Rev. 1:10). "And thine ears shall hear a word *behind* thee, saying, This [is] the way, walk ye in it" (Is. 30:21).

Even a young child can hear the audible voice of God. Just like the boy Samuel (1 Sam. 3:9), you don't have to be super spiritual, famous, or mature to hear from the Lord. Notice the process: 1) Samuel thought this voice sounded familiar (like Eli's). 2) Samuel didn't recognize that voice as being God. 3) Samuel learned how to recognize the voice of God. Through childlike faith, you listen and learn to hear.

You can be LED through the AUDIBLE VOICE that others can also hear. New Christians usually imagine that they will always hear the thundering voice of God all the time. While this is sometimes possible, it isn't typical. Audible voices will not be the main way you communicate with the Lord.

- A Divine audible voice causes spiritual vibrations that allow spiritually tuned people to hear. Remember, a spiritually manifested voice requires spiritual sensitivity and spiritual discernment to perceive (Acts 9:1-9, 22:9).

You are "LED" through VERBAL PROPHETIC COMMUNICATION. All these VERBAL operations are spontaneous and with no pre-meditation, as the Holy Spirit brings the utterance. They normally seem to bypass the mind and come directly out of the mouth. Your vocalization of Godly Gifts is a witness that edifies the church. Verbal communication is one of many ways you express and articulate the anointing of God.

Prophecy is the Gift of God moving in you and through you for the edification of others.

You can be LED prophetically by the WORD OF KNOWLEDGE. The spiritual gift of the WORD OF KNOWLEDGE is the perception of a portion of certain facts from the mind of God to a believer. The Word of Knowledge is always conveyed supernaturally and spontaneously, perhaps during prayer, dreams, visions, revelation, or an audible voice.

This gift can tell the whereabouts, conditions, nature, or thoughts of a person even when it's impossible to know that in the natural. It looks into the heart, mind, or nature of a person to reveal secrets and intentions (see Acts 9:11-16; 10:9-17).

CAUTION: This gift can be diagnostic, telling you what is happening or what has happened. It may uncover the past. As with all gifts, and particularly this one, *caution* should be used to avoid embarrassing someone in public. The purpose is to bring edification and comfort.

HOW TO BE LED

We have the more sure word of prophecy. (2 Peter 1:19, see also Genesis 40:8).

Wisdom

You can be LED by the WORD of WISDOM – this is a gift from above and not worldly wisdom. This gift is a knowing of the future or interpreting futuristic needs (i.e., famine, disaster, inheritances, etc.). The Word of WISDOM is the spiritual utterance (spoken communication) at a given moment through the Spirit, supernaturally revealing the *mind, purpose* and *plan* of God as applied to a specific situation. The Greek for *word* (in Word of Wisdom) is *logos.*

Prophecy brings us wisdom. It clarifies vision (Prov. 29:18). Wisdom speaks direction and behavior in the future and for specific purposes for later on. These insights can be delivered prophetically.

Tongues

You can be LED by TONGUES. Tongues for private use edifies the one praying.

You can interpret your private tongues for yourself. Oral Roberts taught you to pray in tongues and then using that same "voice" position, immediately begin to speak forth the interpretation. Remember, use your mouth to speak from your SPIRIT and not from your conscious mind!

The Gift of Tongues is a supernatural utterance in a language or languages (earthly or heavenly) which the one doing the speaking does not understand.

It is a miracle of speech (Acts 2:4-8; Acts 8:14; 9:17; 10:46; 19:1-6; 1 Cor. 2:12-14). It is a revelatory gift that is received by faith and stirred up by an act of the will. Tongues supersedes your logical mind and opens spiritual channels of revelation. Tongues "Glorify God." [3]

Private tongues is God speaking in you and through you for the edification of yourself

Tongues is the entrance point to an exchanged Kingdom lifestyle of power and effectiveness. You use them to dispossess strongholds in your mind and take possession of proper thought patterns. Tongues can also provide an entrance for intimacy, connecting prayer, and worship.

Interpretation of Tongues

You can be LED by a public MESSAGE in TONGUES and INTERPRETATION of TONGUES. Paul emphasized that in public arenas, the Gift of Tongues must be interpreted so that everyone could benefit (1 Cor. 14:5).

This process of interpretation of tongues originates out of the spiritual realm – it comes spontaneously out of your belly (you do not consciously

---

3. See my book, "Why I Speak in Tongues!"

process it), and out through your mouth without premeditation, one word at a time.

Tongues is a gift to help you profit (1 Cor. 14:16). God says for you to pray for this gift if you speak with tongues (14:5), and for you all to speak with tongues (14:5, 13).

Paul says that interpretation of tongues is equal to prophecy (I Cor. 14:15). Paul said LET someone interpret (v. 27). There should be SOMEONE to interpret but it does not have to be a CERTAIN one; neither should there be competition (I Cor. 14:27).

- The Gift of Interpretation of Tongues was set in the Church (I Cor. 12).
- This Gift is NECESSARY (v. 22).
- This Gift was never taken out of the Church.
- This Gift was used all down through Church history.
- Paul taught the church at Corinth to use this Gift (I Cor. 14).
- This Gift is not the ability to translate languages, nor is it the repetition of Scripture.

   It interprets the essence of the meaning of tongues into a known language.

Visions

You can be LED through VISIONS. Visions are the visual language of God. Visions are generally seen with the inner eye of the human spirit. That can be when your eyes are wide open – or shut (i.e., 2 Ki. 6:17). Visions are where the heavenly is visible (Ezek. 1:1; Is. 6; Gen. 28:12), and you see into eternal realms (Dan. 8:3, 10:7).

Believers can have visions in the inner-person... perhaps during a quiet time, or study time. Seeing something and interpreting are not the same.

Both Daniel (a seer) and Joseph sought the Lord often to understand the correct interpretation.

For example, Peter saw a "vision" involving unclean food and because of his Jewish customs, he knew that meant to take the Gospel to the Gentiles (Acts 10).

Visions often appear to be "real." Sometimes, they look like moving pictures or a flash of in-SIGHT (like a video or a ticker tape of information).

Ezekiel saw a wheel, Isaiah saw a creature, John saw lamp stands. A vision can be overlaid upon your present surroundings. These may be interpreted for public use in guidance or encouragement, etc.

Visions can often happen WITH a voice out of nowhere. They can address current situations or complexities beyond us. Generally, visions are direct and quite clear to understand.

- INTERNAL VISIONS: Believers can have visions in the *inner person*...perhaps during a quiet time, or study time, or at church. Blinded Saul had an internal/inward vision of Ananias (whom he did not know) coming to help him. These can also be the spontaneous pictures that speak the language of your HEART.

- CLOSED VISIONS: the physical body may fall asleep or fall down as the Spirit moves upon the body.

- EXTERNAL VISIONS: The Spirit of God may communicate to you with pictures that transcend your worldly definition of logic and rational thinking.

- OPEN VISIONS: Paul had an open vision (2 Cor. 12: 2-4) where he could not tell if he was in the body or not. OPEN VISIONS much more advanced and are when we actually see into the spiritual realm (Acts 12:11).

- SPIRITUAL VISIONS: The spirit and the soul join together as one (spirit/souled), like the state of man before the Fall. In this state, God communicates and you remain conscious. This can be a visitation in the realm of heavenly places.

Dreams

You can be LED through DAYDREAMS which are a creation of the Godly imagination. Example: You may sit at home and daydream (like a movie) about what will happen in an upcoming ministry appointment, and later see that come to pass – including the people and content of the message given.

You can be LED through DREAMS. Dreams can speak to you in parabolic and symbolic imagery concerning the ways and intentions of God (Gen. 15:12-17, 20:3, 31, 37, 41:1-32, Dan. 2:1-49, 4:9, 7:1, Is. 29:7, Joel 2:28-29, Job 33:14,15, Matt. 27:19, etc.). Numbers 12:6 say "Hear now I make Myself known to him in a vision; I speak to him in a dream."

Warnings or instruction can come through dreams. Jacob dreamed of angels ascending and descending a ladder. Joseph dreamed about sheaves bowing down. Job 33:15-16 tells us, "In a dream, in a vision of the night, when deep sleep falls upon men, while slumbering on their beds, then He opens the ears of men and seals their instruction..."

Dreams frequently come to you as riddles to figure out. They warn (Dan. 4:5), encourage (Acts 18:9-10), and guide you (Matt. 1:20-21, 2:19-20, 3:13, Acts 16:9). Divinely inspired dreams bring a communion with God (1 Ki. 3:5-15), revelation of Jesus, divine plans for your life (Gen. 37:5), instructions, and revelation. In order to understand them, you need to understand their metaphorical language.

You can deliver messages that come from dreams.

Number 12:6-8, *Hear now make Myself known to him in a vision; I speak to him in a dream.*

The Lord spoke to Moses in visions and dreams – and also face to face, clearly – not in riddles (Num. 12:6-8).

Revelation

You can be LED through REVELATION. Revelation is positional. As you grow and progress, you can hear the next truth. It can come as impressions, pictures, words, etc.

The Greek word for "revelation" means to disclose or to uncover by lifting the curtain and making VISIBLE that which will provide knowledge and understanding into your present reality. It means that God reveals previously unknown truth into you by His Spirit (1 Jn. 2:20). Others don't know until it comes out of your mouth.

Revelation = God imparting His Spirit into your spirit.

Trance

A TRANCE is a cessation or neutralization of present temporal (visual) awareness or natural consciousness (while you are awake) that allows you to perceive another or spiritual visionary co-existing realm where you are not limited (Num. 24, Acts 10:10, 22:17, Rev. 1:10, etc.).

Generally in a trance, the spirit leaves your body (which remains motionless) and you see into heavenly realms. You should not seek having trances and they should not be self-induced. When in a trance, the person is not usually aware of his/her surroundings (Acts 10).

You can experience VISITATIONS in any of the above forms or in real life. Visitations can come from an angel, heavenly messenger, or a form of God that appears to guide or speak. Many New Testament believers benefited from Angelic communications.

You can experience ANGELIC VISITATIONS: Abraham encountered angels. The archangel, Gabriel spoke to Daniel and to Mary because they needed to hear an important message. Many others saw angels as well.

ViSITATION BY THE LORD: Sometimes Jesus reveals Himself to those who love Him (Jn. 14:21).

Angels are highly active in every dimension, every day.

You can experience TRANSPORTATIONS: Transportation (teleportation, translation) happens when a person moves instantly from one location on earth to another place (Acts 8:39, 16:9, Jn. 6:21, etc.). Enoch and Elijah translated and did not return.

You can experience SIGNS AND WONDERS: These demonstrations of His presence may show creativity and infinite power (gold dust, etc.). However, they should only cause you to pay attention to GOD.

You must not follow signs and wonders.

I am blessed to have received songs of the Lord, third heaven experiences, been translocated to other locations, heard the audible voice of God, seen and talked to angels, been physically touched by angels, seen incredible instantaneous miracles, had creative reconstructive healings, experienced demarcations of lines of Glory, bright lights and portals, actual rain indoors for weeks, demagnetized hotel keys, dazzling spectacles, open visions, spiritual visitations, and have had frequent prophetic and seer revelation, etc. THERE IS ONE THING LEARNED FROM THIS: Signs do not LEAD us – they follow us.

YOU MUST NOT follow signs, you follow Christ.

Revelation is not equal in weight or importance but has a progressive increase in validity, accuracy, and clarity.

- Feeling (confirmation).
- Knowing (intuition/insight).
- Vague pictures and impressions (conscience).
- A Word from another church member
- Discernment (good and evil).

- Dreams.

- Twilight (before waking and sleeping).

- Manifestation of the Holy Spirit.

- Word from a recognized, seasoned prophet.

- Trances.

- God's audible voice.

- Visions (literal).

- Visitation (in a vision).

- Visitation of Jesus.

- Heavenly translation.

- Visit from 3rd Heaven.

- Visit from God (blinding white light).

- Throne room experience.

Whatever Gift you seek, that Gift will seek you. Let wisdom flood your being. Prophesy to bring change and order. Prophesy to build up and encourage. Speak life, hope, and peace. Jesus, The Prophet, dwells in you and wants to release you into full expression.

Revealing the Kingdom

The prophetic process is one that needs to inspirationally reveal Kingdom ideas and ideals.

"No prophecy of Scripture is of any private interpretation, for prophecy never comes by the will of man, but holy men of God spoke as they were moved by the Holy Spirit" (1 Pet. 1:19-20). Let inspiration fill you.

Let the Gifts of the Spirit be a great JOY to you.

As for me, I will BEHOLD (see, gaze, look, prophesy) *thy FACE* (countenance) *in righteousness* (that which is just, legal, or prosperous): *I SHALL*

BE SATISFIED (filled and no longer hungry), *when I awake* (OPEN MY EYES) *with thy LIKENESS* (shape, embodiment, manifestation). (Ps. 17:15 KJV)

Beloved Reader,

I sense the stirring of the Spirit to say, "This is not the time to count your yesterdays. Don't look back, but separate from all binding chains.

May you experience in the Lord a complete release - and a NEED to more fully express the World of the Spirit. Here and NOW. This is reality. This moment is an intake, a pouring through of all that Christ is. For He has made preparations. This is your season and moment. Be one of sharp discernment and press through to fill that which pertains to your life."

The Beginning

This booklet partly contains a collection of my notes over 30 years plus there may be information condensed and/or liberally summarized, or conversations, apt phrases, and paraphrases from these specialists listed below.:

Allison, Lora, Conversations

Bickle, Mike, "Beyond Prophesying:" Ministries Today June 1996

Blick, Dick, "River of Power" Social and Spiritual Dimension, Pt. 1

Brownsville Manuals

Brownsville Church Manuals on Church Order

Clark, Jonas, internet articles

Cook, Bruce, "Partnering with Prophetic" Kingdom House Publishing

Early, Tim, "Apostolic Impartation and Prophetic Activation for Your Destiny" ebook

Enliven Blog - Prophesying from Love / ideas – accountability

Fluitt, Clarice, Conversations

Hagin, Kenneth, "The Holy Spirit and His Gifts" Rhema Faith Library,

Jeff, Osage City Foursquare Church, Twin Lakes, Kansas

Life Center Ministries, 2690 Mt. Vernon Rd., Atlanta, GA

Lopez, Jeremy, Conversations and "Releasing the Power of the Prophetic" & "The Eye of the Seer."

Mattera, Joe, *pdf/Understanding 5-fold gifts.*

Spake, Kluane, "Connecting"

Spence, Phil, Notes on "Kingdom Perspective of the Prophetic"

Tay, Roderick, Conversations, interactions

Ministries Today various articles   Pictures are Google images.

CONTACT Dr. Kluane Spake

1- 877-SPAKE-99
spake@mindspring.com

Mail: P.O. Box 941933   Atlanta, GA 31141   http://kluane.com

Dr. Kluane Spake has spent a lifetime teaching and training leaders and believers on how to apply the word to their daily lives and how to maximize their potential relevance and effectiveness.

She is a Commissioned Ambassadorial Apostle and is internationally recognized as an apostle, minister, author, mentor, scholar, educator, and friend to the Body of Christ. Dr. K is a pastor to pastors and mentor. She is Founder of SWORD Ministries, Jubilee Alliance Apostolic Network.

Dr. Kluane's greatest mandate is to release the "Revealing of Christ in a People" and to awaken the full benefits of Salvation. Her articles are circulated widely across the world. And she desires to release a balanced and scripturally sound approach to prophetic ministry.

She has ministered to thousands overseas and around the world, including Guam, across Philippines, Indonesia, Hong Kong, Kuala Lumpur, mainland China, Bahamas, Virgin Islands, Singapore, Australia, Solomon Islands (photo above), Alaska, Hawaii, across the US and Canada, and etc. She has also been the guest on several radio and TV programs.

She is the author of several nationally published books and founder of "The School of the Apostles."   http://kluane.com

Here are a few of our other books by Dr. K also available for you"

"40 Day Focus on Prosperity" A 40 day study on Biblical prosperity..

"From Enmity to Equality" A comprehensive & scholarly study on women and Christianity

"Whole & Holy" Imparting a passionate longing for Christ-like image and likeness.

"Understanding Headship" A booklet concerning the accurate concepts of headship.

"Finding Wisdom" A book describing how to achieve personal fulfillment.

"Connecting" How to apprehend spiritual realities.

"Why I Speak in Tongues!" A practical book on speaking in tongues.

"Angel's Friends & Curriculum" A Children's book and curriculum on gender and racial equality.

"Melchizedek King Priest" One of the most important studies you will ever undertake to reign in life with ever-increasing dominion.

"Finding Health to Fulfill Your Destiny" A journey into the world of disease-preventing nutrition.

"Identity is Everything!" My Preaching Notes on Identity!

"Understanding Headship" E-Book, An easy to understand booklet explaining the correct Scriptural understanding of "headship."

"Gold Fever" An autobiographical novel about adventures in the arctic!

Please go to http://kluane.com and sign up for my monthly newsletter and Check out "The School of the Apostles!"

Dr. Kluane - SWORD, P.O.Box 941933, Atlanta, GA 31141

Made in the USA
Middletown, DE
19 September 2021